A Hero's Journey To Healthy Leadership

Martina Violetta Jung

A Hero's Journey To Healthy Leadership

1st edition published by Healing Stories – Martina Jung

Bahnstrasse 22, 40822 Mettmann, Germany

Printed by CreateSpace, An Amzaon.com Company,

4900 LaCross Road, North Charleston, SC 29406, USA

www.createspace.com

Available from Amazon.com and other book stores. Available on Kindle and other devices.

Cover design by Kirsten Lenz

Edited by Johanna Ellsworth

ISBN-10: 1532830971
ISBN-13: 978-1532830976

DEDICATION

I dedicate my creation to Pope Francis, who shows us every day that healthy leadership is not about being perfect. It is about living what love, human dignity and accountability are about.

CONTENTS

Acknowledgments

The Story 1

Epilogue 179

The Author 183

ACKNOWLEDGMENTS

My deepest gratitude does to

Prof. Dr. Erny Gillen, Stephanie Ehrenschwendner, Martin G. Hess, Virginie Issumo, Jean-Luc Karleskind, Sharon K. Richards, Dr. Kerstin Vogel and Julia Zhang-Zedrosser for making valuable suggestions to improve the manuscript;

Johanna Ellsworth for editing;

Kirsten Lenz of sonnendeckgrafik in Cologne for designing the cover; and to

Sharon K Richards for permitting me to quote and publish two poems of her latest collection Word Song from My Soul II.

Martina Violetta Jung April 2016

CHAPTER 1

"Damn," Martin shouted and hit the horn on the black leather steering wheel with the palm of his sweaty right hand. He considered this a crucial day for his desperately awaited career move from Senior Vice President into the Executive Committee of the company, and now he was stuck in a stupid traffic jam. Martin looked at his wristwatch, the one he had carefully selected from his beloved collection of Swiss-made chronographs this morning. It was already 8:23 am. No way would he make it on time to the meeting with the Strategic Task Force Next Generation Leaders installed by the new CEO. And even if he still made that meeting, he would surely be late for the CEO's address to the international top management at 10 am in the auditorium. That meeting was decisive for his career step. Martin pushed the phone button and selected the short dial for his assistant, Karin Bach.

"Good morning, Dr. Fox."

"Good morning, Karin. Listen, I'm stuck in a traffic jam – can you call my deputy and tell him to excuse myself with the young managers? I want to get there in time for the CEO's address so I can catch a front row seat."

"You can't do that! Word will surely reach the CEO. And don't forget: it was you who sent these young managers a mail reminding them about their duty to the company and –"

"Fair point. Let me think about how to manage this – "

"I have the Chief Financial Officer India on the other line right now. He desperately wants to talk to you. Can I put him through?"

"As if this was important now," Martin muttered.

"What did you say, Dr. Fox? The connection seems fuzzy."

"Alright, put him through."

"Doctor Fox, good morning from India."

"Good Morning Mr. Singh. Could you keep it short, please?"

"I need your okay for the extension of the specialities production line in Chennai. Everbody has given a go, and Mr. Kirch is pushing to start building as of the next week."

"I haven't had the time to look at the revised investment plan yet. As I understand it differs from what the Board of Directors has agreed to."

"The only major difference is that we have reduced costs. Our financials are very tight. You know that better than I."

Martin needed to concentrate hard when listening to his caller's Indian accent. Why did they hardly open their mouths and kept everything on the same pitch level?

"I'll give you my answer within the next two weeks."

"But it must be on your desk for at least six weeks already now."

Do you really believe, Martin thought, that I'll have my arch rival Mr. Kirch score points now and make it to the ExCom instead of me?

"Dr. Fox, are you still there?"

"Yes, and I have nothing more too add."

"I can't accept your answer," he replied in a staccato voice. "If you don't find a way to give me your okay by tomorrow, you force me to bring this to the attention of my Country Manager and Mr.

Kirch."

"Do as you please." Martin clenched his jaw while hanging up.

Martin rang Joseph Mayer, his second in command.

"Good Morning, Mayer, I'll be late for the meeting with the youngsters that starts now."

"By how much?"

"Can't say, traffic jam."

"How do you want me to proceed?"

"What is the exact topic of the meeting?"

"The Strategic Task Force Next Generation Leaders have to explore – wait, I need to check Dr. Bergan's mail to give you the exact wording – (1) new ways of how we do business, (2) new methods of judging our performance."

"OK, Mayer. Welcome them and pretend to help them as best as you can. Find out what they are up to, but don't share any of the hot projects and acquisitions we have in the pipeline until I get there."

"But, Dr. Fox, the new CEO told us that our long-standing company values – Respect, Transparency, Honesty, and Cooperation - are non-negotiable any more."

"You don't need to remind me, Mayer. But you need to understand 'values are for show, tactics are for dough'. Who shall run the company if all key players have to be kicked out because we act against our values? Come on, Mayer, get real – "

"You're probably right, Dr. Fox –"

"I am, as always. Mayer, listen, if I make it into the ExCom now, you'll succeed me. We have to stick together here and everything will work out just fine."

"I understand."

When Martin rang off, he had a wide smile on his face. Up to the useful tricks of sabotaging again. He rubbed his chin and then smoothed his tie.

The phone rang again, interrupting Martin's thoughts of how he could best impress the new CEO during his speech today. He looked at the display.

"Yes, Helen, what is it?"

"You forgot your pills."

"What pills?" Martin said, pinching his lips together.

"The ones your doctor prescribed on Monday to control your blood pressure, cholesterol and reflux. It is Thursday today, have you already forgotten? You're just forty-eight, not eighty-four."

"My health is really not the issue today." His voice got strained. "It's my chance of making it to the 'Senior C Suite', the ExCom, don't you get it? I've worked my butt off for years to grab such an opportunity when it comes along. If I don't make it now, I might be too old when the next opportunity comes up. This is my chance – or I'll stay sandwiched between ExCom and Vice Presidents for the rest of my bloody career."

"Well, if you think so..." His wife hung up as if nothing had happened.

Martin's nostrils flared. When would she ever understand what was really going on in the company? His stomach pushed some acidic breakfast bits up his gullet. No, I'm being unfair, he thought. Helen cares about our son and me. He decided to apologize to her by text message once the meeting with the CEO was over. His gaze wandered off into the mirror. The knot of his handmade shiny red silk tie was perfect and in place. He turned the knob of the music function to pick a song to keep his mind occupied while sparkling spring sunlight danced on the windshield and into the car. Skyfall. Yes, that seamed the right song now.

Bling bling. Martin looked at the text message. "Can leave my office early today. CU hotel FH, Room 312, 7:30 pm? xxx". He licked his lips, smiled and texted: "OK."

Delightfully Martin opened the black leather-covered armrest of his BMW 5 full option, took out the little golden box that had the shape of a raging bull, picked one of the little white pills and swallowed it with a smile on his face and wide-open eyes. ExCom, here I come, he thought before drifting away in thoughts of replacing this car with a chauffeur driven Mercedes S class with a mahogany-lined interior. Finally, he would be able to add some even more exclusive pieces to his Swiss chronographs collection, too. His eyes sparkled in anticipation.

CHAPTER 2

"Where are they, Karin?" Martin asked, rushing into his office and looking around.

"The Members of the Strategic Work Force Next Generation Leaders?"

"Who else?"

"In Mr. Mayer's office."

"Listen, go to the auditorium and place one of the leadership books from my shelf on a chair in the first row."

"Any particular book?"

"Hmmm – take Winning by Jack Welch."

"Dr. Bergan already sent a hand-out for the meeting."

Martin looked at his watch again.

"It's 9.27 am now. Go down to the auditorium right away and send me a text message to confirm that everything is fine. Print the hand-out later and put it in my briefcase."

Martin left for Mr. Mayer's office in a hurried step, knocked on the door and entered without waiting for a reply.

"Dr. Fox, great that you could still make it; we have some thirty minutes left," Mr. Mayer said to Martin while standing up to shake his hand.

"Sorry for being late, guys. I had an unexpected and urgent one-on-one with the CEO before the top management meeting. And I have to leave you again in twenty minutes at the latest." Martin looked at his watch. He hadn't intended to tell this lie; it had just slipped out of his mouth.

The three young people remained silently seated but rolled their eyes, as did Mr. Mayer. Then the young man sitting across from Martin started to tap his fingers on the table. The Western-looking woman to his left crossed her arms in front of her chest with a tight expression on her face, and the Asian-looking young woman to his right looked at Martin with cold, hard brown eyes. Before Mr. Mayer could introduce Emma Cunningham, Zhang Ai, and Thomas Winter, to Martin, he pointed his finger at the young man and claimed, "I know you. You are a BU controller, considered a bright, system-cracking nerd. And you are the nephew of the Chairman of the Works Council, right?"

Thomas Winter was a well-built young man, five foot six, with light brown, rather curly hair and a round boyish face with big green eyes. His features were finely chopped, yet a gripping purposefulness was written all over his face. He wore a dark blue suit and a white shirt with an open collar.

"You don't know me, Dr. Fox, I can assure you of that," he replied in a nasal voice with a sharp undertone. "But I can't deny that Franz Winter happens be my uncle."

"Didn't your meeting go well so far?" Martin asked, looking at Mr. Mayer.

"None of our questions got answered, if that's what you mean, Dr. Fox? But it would be oh so kind of you to have the courtesy now," Thomas replied sarcastically.

Bling bling, a text message from Karin. It didn't work out. Can you come outside Mr. Mayer's office for a moment?

Martin ran his right hand through his hair. "Sorry guys, this is more important right now." He stood up and left the room again.

Karin was waiting for him outside, fiddling with her long brown hair.

"What do you mean, Karin? It is quite simple – just enter the room, place the book, and leave the room. It was still half an hour before the CEO's speech is due to commence. Don't tell me all front-row seats were already taken. Who dares to sit there besides the CFO and Karl Kirch anyway?"

"Well, with George, I mean Dr. Bergan – Sorry, but it takes time for me to get used to addressing our CEO by first name and without his title. We're a traditional German chemicals company, gell?" Karin started to fan air to her flushed face.

"Karin, come to the point."

"Yes, what I wanted to say is that I couldn't place the book because we have a different breed of boss now, and what magic eyes he has," she said with glowing cheeks and a yearning look in her eyes.

"Karin, is there something wrong with you today?"

"No, I'm quite all right, just confused. Can you believe it? George stood at the door, welcoming each participant personally before entering the auditorium. He also turned to me as I waited in line. He recognized me as your assistant, even knew my name, can you believe it? He asked whether he could be of help. I just said I was looking for you. He replied that he had not seen and welcomed you yet. But if necessary, he'd pass a message. Politely, I declined and left. Or should I have told him what my real task was?"

"No – surely not. Thanks, Karin," Martin grumbled. He turned around on his left heel and went back into Mr. Mayer's office.

Martin returned to his chair absent-mindedly. Frowning, he leaned back and crossed his arms in front of his chest without saying anything for a moment while everyone was staring at him. He looked at his wristwatch: 9:45 am.

"Sorry, guys, we need to make a new appointment. But before I dismiss you, there is one more thing you could tell me in a few short sentences."

If I can't sit in George's field of vision now, Martin thought, I can at least shine with some first-hand information from the younger generation.

The three young managers stared at each other in disbelief. But before one of them was quick-witted enough to stop Martin, he continued, "I have heard from our HRM Asia last week that five high potentials of your generation have left the company last months. What's your generation's problem with being loyal to this company?"

Emma got furious and jumped at the question, flushing. "We are not loyal to this company any more because the company is not loyal to us! And with company I mean its top management, people like you."

"Never mind Emma," Thomas turned to his two team mates, shielding his mouth with his hand so only they could hear him. "He's a Muggle, without any imagination or magic to move things."

"Oh," Martin blurted.

"Yes." Emma stayed focused on Martin. "We get paid less than the generation before us. Many of us don't get fixed contracts but just temporary ones. We get less benefits and security. All of that happens because your generation is taking care of themselves first and foremost. What matters are your pensions, your benefits and your positions. You don't care about anyone else and their needs." Emma's voice started to crack but she forced herself to go on. "This is what the twelve of us in this Strategic Task Force Next Generation Leaders observe in each country. And in some countries it is even worse. Our generation is merely considered junior cannon fodder."

"Mr. Fox," Thomas added, "our generation believes in sharing. We in this Task Force are already blessed by being brighter than most at our age and have received a fine education. We know we're privileged and take responsibility for those less fortunate yet with different skills. For example, when we go and buy glasses, we buy two. One for us and one for somebody who can't afford it but needs it, too. And –"

Martin moved towards the table. He pointed his finger at the three and interrupted Thomas.

"I'm sorry but I don't buy that talk about sharing wealth and riches someone has worked for very hard to make strangers happy and feeling equal. We are not equal. The very reason why you sit here means you are better than others. You stand out, even among your peers."

"We don't intend to stand out, Mr. Fox. We have the ambition to contribute," Emma jumped into the conversation again.

"Anyway," Martin continued and leaned forward even more, "we're living in a market economy. It has proven superior to anything that communist or Marxist style romantics have ever invented, ignoring a human being's inner drives. And market economy is about fierce competition, about survival of the fittest, and in consequence the better ones get more, live better, survive longer. Face it."

"We disagree with your definition of what equality is about," Emma replied, grinding her teeth.

Martin rolled his eyes angrily. How dared they challenge him like that? He was Senior Vice President and they were still nobodies.

"In our definition, Mr. Fox, equality means oneness despite being diverse. We respect each other as individuals with different capabilities, views and needs, yet perceive each other as members of one human family. It is our essence as human beings that makes us equal – not our abilities, nationalities and what we can contribute to the whole. Here we are very different indeed. But as we only have one Earth as one common home for all human beings, we take care that everyone's needs are met."

"I haven't booked a lecture in equality," Martin replied, frowning while straightening his tie.

"And I ask you to let me finish what I have to say," Emma countered in a strained voice, lifting her chin. "The socialist thinkers of various backgrounds have defined equality as the abolition of exploitation, the use of man by another man, regardless whether this was cruel or human. They were focused on creating material equality, which doesn't work. We all know that. In our capitalistic world the meaning of equality has been transmuted. To top managers like you 'equality' has become 'sameness'. And sameness you fear, because you cannot feel appreciated without being able to stand out. And to stand out, you compete, cheat, lie, smash others, take more than you actually need and show off with things you can buy to set you apart from others. But what you have become are men without any individuality whatsoever. You need labels, goods and memberships to pretend you have individuality. But who you are, what your capabilities are that make you unique, you have forgotten. You can't feel the unity with other human being any more."

Martin felt a flush of pain in his stomach. He felt as if he had just lost a fight, not the whole battle, but one serious fight. He couldn't despise this young woman, but he hated how she had exposed his superficiality.

"Who are you?" he wanted to know from Emma.

"I'm a woman, a mother of a two-year-old girl who needs to have a life worth living as well and, if this is what you mean, I'm an engineer, production manager of our plant in Houston, and I also have a degree in philosophy."

Martin looked over to Mr. Mayer, pulling at his tight shirt collar while grimacing. "You're too young and idealistic to act responsibly. Real life will catch you sooner or later," Martin fired back, straightening his shoulders.

"Who knows." Thomas raised his eyebrows and gave him a glassy stare. "At least it's crystal clear to us that it's because of people like you, who care about themselves more than about anything else, that our company is in trouble now.

CHAPTER 3

The auditorium was packed with some 200 top managers from around the globe. When Martin entered the room, still painfully digesting Thomas' accusation, he pulled out his white shirt cuffs from underneath his dark blue jacket and checked whether the silver cufflinks shaped like dragons were in their proper place. To his frustration he could only find a seat in the very back of the room. He stood up again to check out who was sitting close to George in the first row. Something was in the air – that was for certain. The Chairman of the Board, Mr. Kennedy, an elderly Irish gentleman, was present, and a woman Martin had never seen before sat between George and the Chairman. Martin put both hands in his pockets and watched.

Generous applause filled the room when George left his seat. With a spring in his step he moved up the stairs, taking two at a time, to claim centre stage. A young man followed him and switched on his pre-arranged head set microphone. There he stood, looking at the audience, relaxed, his feet evenly balanced on the planks. George wasn't what one would call handsome, at least from Martin's point of view. He was five foot seven, with a well-trained, slender body and short yet full dark-blond hair that was turning grey around the ears. His oval face had wrinkles near his mouth and eyes, whereas his rimless glasses provided an intellectual touch to his appearance. What had impressed Martin was his education, which looked the same as his own but wasn't. Georg Bergan had obtained a degree in Chemistry from Cambridge University and a Doctoral Degree in Chemistry from the ETH in Zurich. Martin graduated in Chemistry from Munich University and his Ph.D. was rather due to the connection he had via his beating frat. George's career path, by contrast, didn't impress Martin all that much. George had made a line management career with two well-respected companies. First with a major energy provider in Norway and later with a world-class chemical company in the U.S. But interestingly, nobody knew what had happened to him in the last three years; not even Google had been able to provide answers to Martin's questions. Little was known about George Bergan's private life, too. In his introduction to the company some three months ago it had said that he was fifty-five years of age, had a German mother and a Norwegian father, was remarried to a woman of Belgian descent and the father of two girls in their late twenties from his first marriage to an American woman.

As nearly every day when Martin had met with him before, George was wearing a dark grey suit, a light blue button-down shirt with the first button open, black shoes with rubber soles, a belt of the same colour and a simple golden wedding ring. The CEO looked at the audience with a friendly smile while Martin remembered their meetings. George had listened to his views and strategy suggestions for nearly five hours during the last couple of weeks. On top of that, they had met in various meetings related to mergers and acquisitions. Martin took his hands out of his pockets again to dry-wash them in anticipation of what George would say now.

"Great moments, my friends, are born from great opportunities." George started opening his arms towards the audience. "And such a great opportunity is right in front of us now. Why? We are just short of having nothing to loose any more." People looked at each other, stunned. George pulled his arms back, put his left hand on his stomach and raised his right arm half-way again while continuing to speak. "The catastrophic numbers in our balance sheet, our actuals and in our forecast tell only a fraction of the story. The fraction we permit ourselves to look at. But that won't help us survive. Our survival is not primarily in the numbers, it's not in our technological leadership, it's not in our long-standing German brand name, it's not in another cost-saving round and more lay-offs of blue-collar workers around the world." George closed his right hand but lifted his index finger up to the ceiling. "No. Our survival is in embracing reality. Today's reality is more important than past ideas we hold dear."

People shook their heads and began to mutter. Martin had expected that George would tell them that the situation was seriously difficult but not life-threatening if they all put in some extra hours and focus more on squeezing the last Euros out of everything. That they needed to keep their commodity business alive and at minimal cost while building on ever new speciality production units with higher margins, protecting their intellectual property like hell, and that they should seriously investigate upstream or downstream integrations. None of that! Hadn't George listened to him at all? To Martin the solution was so damn obvious: just applied business school knowledge.

"My friends, a healthy future for the company and by that for all of us, for all our people and partners, for our owners and potential investors depends on whether we will be able to become the master of reality and two things in particular that threaten to kill us now. On the one hand," George said, stretching out his right arm, "there are sick leadership behaviours, attitudes and habits in our company that threaten our very future with every word we speak and every action we take because they're not interacting with the total reality. On the other hand," he stretched out his left arm, "we operate out of an organisational structure suitable to be placed in a museum of industrialisation but totally inadequate for the age of information and digitalisation where the domination of certain nationalities and borders as means of separation have proven to be a deadly illusion." George brought both palms together in front of his chest, fingers directed to the ceiling. "Add to that, my friends, resources that have become ever more scarce, air, water and soils ever more polluted, and that there is little left we have to offer to generations that will follow us. Now you know what we will have to master."

He paused and let his arms sink again. Martin flushed. He rubbed his neck with his right hand while looking at George, who put one foot forward and lifted his arms again like a conductor going for a crescendo.

"The responsibility to lead under these circumstances is not a privilege. It is a heavy burden, demanding humility and sacrifices. A burden, only bearable by mature and healthy leaders. You can become such leaders. At the moment, most of you are not. I know you don't like to hear that. But I haven't taken this job because I want or need your applause and approval. I have accepted this position to shake things up and tear down whatever walls there are in our heads and in our organisation that hold us back from facing reality. Our main shareholders have decided on a path that will secure a rewarding future for all involved, not just for the ones at and near the top of the hierarchy. We need to find and walk a path that has not been trod before by a chemical company, a path that will respect all human beings as well as our planet. The first step on this path is to face all facts and acknowledge them. That is what I intend to do with you here today." George dropped his arms and looked at them.

A harsh murmur went through the auditorium. Martin dragged his hand through his hair and straightened his tie in disbelief of what he had just heard. Narrowing his eyes, he looked at George.

"Together with the members of the Executive Committee," George continued, "you are considered the top men and women leading this company. You've all received substantial leadership education, trainings and coaching. But so far most of you are only great as long as you manage numbers, selected facts, technical questions and your own desires. We have to do a lot better if we want to keep this company in business."

Martin tugged at his tie and started to sweat. He was pissed, to say the least. How dared George attack him and his colleagues like that? He made a fist with his right hand and kneaded it with his other one before putting both hands into his trouser pockets. Everyone around him started to whisper indignantly.

"Mature and healthy leadership, my friends, begins with self-leadership. And the key to self-leadership is self-awareness. You need to know exactly what your strengths are. You need to know exactly what your weaknesses are. All those hidden thoughts, beliefs and habits that keep you from fully utilizing your strengths. And you need to know exactly what values and worldviews you've been ignoring along the way. Let me ask you this: Who considers himself self-aware according to these four pillars?"

Martin pulled his left hand out of his trouser pocket and rubbed his cheek. He noticed that no arm went straight up. A few people hesitantly lifted their arms but stopped half-way as if they were having serious doubts. Martin had not even considered lifting his arm.

"Good," George said, nodding. "I see that you agree there is work at hand." He paused. "Mature and healthy leadership requires three more things. Number one is to innovate confidently and constantly, embracing a world changing by the minute. And by that I mean to innovate and embrace change on all levels and in all aspects of the company, including yourselves, the way you work, the structures in which you work and the procedures you follow. Number two is to engage with all others with a loving and caring attitude. You need to believe in the abilities and willingness of everyone to contribute something meaningful and go out of your way for them to live it. Number three is to energize yourselves and others through heroic ambitions. The ambition as such is not what I consider heroic, but the attitude with which you live it. In today's world, these ambitions need to differ from the ones we've considered worthwhile for so many decades. In the past, we sent out people from Germany into the world to conquer it and fulfil our needs. The German perspective prevailed, the German needs were superior. Now we need to have the ambition to mobilize all our abilities worldwide in an equal manner. And in going forward we need to heal the wounds we once inflicted with our past behaviours."

Martin started to sweat even more as he saw his rival Karl Kirch standing up. Karl was the Head of Business Unit Specialty Chemicals, a tall, imposing man with the eyes of a machine gunner, a former karate fighter. He said in a deep voice, "You talk like a politician, George. I'm more concerned with achieving tangible results fast. This is what we need now to get us out of our red numbers."

And though I don't want you to score points, Martin thought, I have to agree with you on that.

"Do you believe in continuous improvement, Karl?" George returned the challenge.

"Sure I do."

"Who else does? Raise your arms, please."

Martin lifted his right arm, and everyone else raised their arms as well.

"Can you improve if you don't change anything?"

Martin and many more shook their heads.

"Do you know what the definition of insanity is, Karl?"

Martin stared at George with wide eyes.

"It's insane to continue to do things as you have always done and hope for better results just by hiring a new CEO."

Martin cleared his throat, rubbed the palms of his sweaty hands together and challenged him as well by asking, "But, George, how will we fill our bank accounts right now?"

"Mature and healthy leaders are able to build healthy relationships. Relationships in which you serve others – employees, customers, shareholders, business partners – by meeting their legitimate needs while treating them with dignity, respect, humility and kindness."

"I can't follow you any more, George," Karl interjected. "If I gave people all they want, then we are done and dusted."

"Listen more carefully, Karl. It's not about what people want, it's about what their legitimate needs are. And you have to make sure that all legitimate needs are met. So far we are doing poorly in that respect. We tick the boxes of the individual wants of a few people at the higher end of the hierarchy and let everyone else pay the bill, right?"

"No," quite a few in the auditorium countered loudly as if they had been attacked personally, including Martin and Karl.

"Let me challenge you all." George raised his right hand again and lifted his voice. "What would you think of your leadership if you had to work for our company as a blue-collar worker in Germany, in India, in Brazil, in South Africa or any other country you might think of? I don't expect you to answer that right now, but I expect you to seriously reflect on it."

An awkward atmosphere developed in the room. The hair on Martin's nape and arms bristled while his shoulders began to tighten.

"But how do we fill our bank accounts right now, George?" Martin asked once more. He saw Peter Stark, the CFO, nodding emphatically in the first row.

"Human relationships resemble bank accounts, Martin. You make a deposit when you serve others and treat them as you wish to be treated. And you make a withdrawal when you take more than you need and leave the other with less than they need. Over time, those who are always at the losing end will be a lot less committed or even leave the relationship. Let me ask everybody here in this room: How many customers have we lost because we didn't perform well in the last two years? How many great people have left the company during that time because their ideas on how to change things were ignored? How many business partners have we lost because we squeezed them like a lemon?"

People looked at each other in acknowledgement of serious overdrafts. Martin loosened his tie and opened the top button of his shirt.

"Let me tell you how I see it. The relationship bank accounts of our company are empty. Some are even deeply in the red and have been that for quite some time. Our financial problems are but a consequence of that."

A loud murmur filled the room; it sounded like ocean waves on a stormy day. Martin turned to the wall and started to walk up and down with his thoughts running wild.

"During my conversations and meetings with you in the last

three months I was able to observe behavioural patterns that don't allow a leader to build healthy relationships and thereby keep the bank accounts of the company filled. I call these behaviour patterns sick. They've gotten hold of so many of you that one could talk of a contagious epidemic that is taken for granted without being noticed any more." George paused, looking around. "It is the thoughts, feeling and actions of all the people that make a company. And it's the leaders who set the tone for that. So when the leaders are sick, the whole company gets sick." He paused once more and looked at his listeners, many of whom shook their heads.

"OK, you want proof? You get it." George accepted the challenge. "Our latest Employer Branding Survey confirms this in numbers. 'Lack of adequate Leadership' is our most burning in-house risk. Check the results on the intranet if you haven't done so yet."

Martin exhaled deeply and looked down. He was aware of the devastating numbers that George was dangling right under the nose of everybody like him in leadership positions.

George clapped his hands together. "I've made an effort to cluster the sick behaviour patterns I have observed in five groups. I have given these sick behaviour patterns memorable names, I hope: The Egocentrics, the Workaholics, the Heart-of-Stone Guys, the Self-Forgotten and the Masked. A hand-out was sent to you earlier this morning, and it has been published on the intranet. These sick behaviour patterns need to go for good, my friends. They keep us from having a future that is desirable, healthy, safe and sustainable for everyone involved."

Martin's eyes became dull and lifeless. He looked down and let his arms sink until his left hand reached for the handkerchief in his pocket to wipe the sweat from his brow.

"Let me just introduce you to the most damaging sick behaviours of the Egocentrics." George continued but Martin didn't want to hear it. "The Egocentrics are people who perceive themselves as immune, indispensable, superior or even immortal. They aspire power, positions, profits and perks. They are eager to put themselves on display. To stand out as more capable and successful than others, they may use any means. They are ambitious and boastful. They define their place in the world through status symbols and medals of honour. It's all about what they get, not what they contribute. Please raise your hands now if you recognize these behaviours among our top managers."

More than eighty percent of his listeners slowly lifted their hands while looking around as if they were searching for confirmation from others. Martin sat down, shaking his head wildly in disbelieve. He couldn't understand why George had any problems with that. That's how things worked in a big company like theirs. You had to stand out in order to be noticed and get your fair share of the cake. The higher you moved up in the hierarchy, the bigger the stakes and higher the rewards.

"Until today many of you might probably have thought that this is simply the change of strategy under a new CEO to get back to black figures and an attempt to regain the attention and respect of investors, customers and the public at large. Well, it isn't! We're here to give our company – and the whole industry – a new direction. Time has come to reinvent ourselves. The cornerstone of this is what the chairman, Mr. Kennedy, calls a Three Generations Perspective. In everything we decide and do, we will picture the potential consequences for ourselves, our children, our grandchildren on a global level."

"And you want our opinion on that, George?" Karl Kirch asked, challenging him once again. Karl didn't have any children, and his wife had divorced him because he played incessantly Poker. What do you know, Karl, Martin thought, his own son, Christopher, in mind. Of course Martin wanted his son's life to be great, at least as great as his own, if not better.

"No," replied George firmly, "the Board of Director's Three Generations Perspective is a given fact. You can decide to join this new vision and way of looking at ourselves and the industry at large. Or you can decide to keep your current view, but then it will be hard to find a suitable position for you."

The audience exhaled collectively. Martin started to sweat all over. Did George really mean that? Broaden your perspective beyond what you are taking into account today – or no future for you in this company?

"My friends, please consider this to be a serious invitation to co-shape our future by reinventing ourselves and our company. Work on yourselves and contribute actively in the various groups and dialog forums that will look in detail at how we need to transform our company's structure, its procedures and control mechanisms as well as how we can better judge our own performance on the road ahead to get in tune with reality. As most of you know, I have installed a Strategic Task Force Next Generation Leaders. Please do your utmost to support them whenever they ask for your input."

Martin recollected himself, stood up again and said in a loud voice, "I guess then you'll have to fire many who are in this room right now." Many listeners turned around and stared at him while he was standing in the back, flushed and sweaty. His stomach hurt. "No", replied George even more firmly than before, "there's no need to fire anyone who suffers from narrow-minded views and sick behavior patterns at this point."

"Well, then you've lost me, George," Martin said in a trembling voice. "What you're telling us is that most of us don't do what is needed in our jobs, that we're in fact responsible for the current situation of our company because we ignore a substantial part of reality, but you don't want to fire us. How does that fit together?"

"Thank you, Martin, for addressing that. I really appreciate that you dare to put the stinking fish on the table so that we can talk about it openly."

Wow. Martin and many others were impressed. It looked like this guy knew what he was up to and well prepared.

"The way you behave was acceptable until today. I can't hold that against you. But it's no longer good enough. Reality is more complex, uncertain, volatile and ambiguous than our current structures, processes, control mechanisms and ideas that cling to a past glory can comprehend. So we need to rely on the abilities of all our employees everywhere in the world much more than ever before. To do that, we need leaders who are able and willing to comprehend and act accordingly. People suffering from sick behavior patters are not capable of doing that."

Martin exhaled deeply. His gaze became empty while looking at George.

"The main shareholders have made a conscious decision to pick a chairman and support his choice of a new CEO, two people who don't fit the current system of the company. Mr. Kennedy walked his own path throughout his entire career, relying on what was right to do for humanity first and foremost, putting his own livelihood at risk where necessary. I walked a more classical career path in two large and well-established companies, only to mature and become myself after having failed miserably on a professional and on a private level. It was this humbling experience of failure, facing it and fixing what was wrong with me that qualified me for the CEO position."

People looked at each other, irritated, to say the least. Martin shook his head. How could George say something like that? No one would ever admit failure voluntarily.

"As of today, my friends, we start a new era in the history books of this company. Our values will guide our actions. Combined with our Three Generations Perspective and with more detailed specifications we will have to develop together, they will be the essence of our joint efforts. What I'm asking of you now is to develop your character and become self-aware with great care and attention. Get rid of any of the sick behavior patterns that stand in your and therefore in our company's way. End egocentric and workaholic behavior patterns. Dissolve the heart of stone in your chest and revitalize the heart that beats. Drop your masks, whatever they might be. Turn to the self-forgotten part of you and start living it."

"And how long do you give us to do all that, George?" Martin interjected, using his last resources.

"I will be patient and support you as long as it takes, provided you are committed and honest. But if you try to play games with me to prolong your current ways of doing, I will become tough on you, my friends. Because that way the well-being and the future of the whole is at highest risk. I don't mind if you make mistakes, but I expect you to admit to them and to do your utmost to make amends, especially if your actions or omissions have hurt others." George exhaled deeply and opened his arms widely. "There is room for all of you who heal themselves from sick behavior patterns, open up to today's realities and collaborate to secure this company's future together. So let's do it, my friends!"

George bowed like a conductor of an orchestra after he had finished his performance. Martin sat down. He felt pain in his chest and a little dizzy. George left the stage with a short and mild applause while Mr. Kennedy went to meet him half-way to shake hands.

At first sight Mr. Kennedy seemed like a jolly old Irish man. Not only Martin thought so, especially when he was walking around, handing out his lemon sherbet sweets to everyone with a smile on his face. It was widely known in the company that he had left his home country when he was young, accepting a lot of hardship to seek the opportunities Ireland couldn't offer to him. His red hair had turned grey on his journey, but it was still full and framed his gentle face, as did his beard. Today he wore a dark blue corduroy jacket and sunflower-yellow corduroy trousers with a button-down shirt in blue, red and white plaid, which pleasantly complemented his appearance. He was also known for the fact that he was a passionate singer and dancer as well as fond of painting abstract landscapes in oil. Some months ago he had told Martin at a reception that these were his exquisite vices. Nothing in the world seemed foreign to his blue eyes behind his red-rimmed bugle glasses. At least that was what Martin believed. You could see his good will and readiness to forgive in these eyes. He had let Martin know discreetly that the worst that could happen to him was that others thought he was rich, for money didn't mean anything to him. But rich he was – in all aspects of life. Mr. Kennedy had made his money by investing in the needs of humanity, spreading permaculture into urban planning, founding eco-villages and a Gaia University for action learning. Martin had once heard a gentleman praise Mr. Kennedy as a man who was able to envision a future that most captains of industry were still blind to see. That, Martin understood, had been the reason why the main investors had asked him to become Chairman of the Board a year ago even though – and this was quite remarkable – he didn't have any knowledge of this industry. They wanted him to re-invent and transform this company as well as the whole chemical industry with his anything-is-possible approach.

Now Martin saw Mr. Kennedy walking across the stage from one end to the other with elated steps, waving his hand, smiling at everyone until he decided it was enough and reached the middle.

"Good day, everybody. Hope you're all well," he said and received a very warm and sustained applause. "I have a dream, and I want to realize it together with you. If life has taught me anything, it's that only the possibility of realizing a dream makes life worth living, exciting and fulfilling. So don't expect me to sit in board meetings as a shareholder of tradition or a subtle administrator of sleepy fate. I have no desire to be popular, although it seems I am," he added with a cheeky grin. People smiled at this, nodded their heads and applauded, as did Martin, although still shaky.

"My dream is to provide well for the next three generations. I call it the Three Generations Perspective. Let that be our common dream. To live our dream, I want you and me to think the unthinkable and do the unheard-of."

Martin's mood lightened up again. He loved thinking he could achieve something great.

"I'm glad," Mr. Kennedy continued, "to inform you that on Board level, we are already making headway. The Company will have an Ethics Experts Committee advising the Board as of tomorrow. This Ethics Experts Committee will review all ethically difficult topics the Board as a whole, I as the Chairman, the CEO or any group of at least ten people from inside the company will put in front of them. That could for example be any question related to investment projects or the reorganization we plan or whether we hire a certain person on top level. In fact, there are very few Ethics Experts available in Europe, and we can call ourselves lucky to have been able to hire a chairwoman for that position who also has several years of experience in change management. Her name is Professor Hannah. In fact, she is excited to join us and build this committee. Whatever is put in front of her and her future colleagues for recommendation and advice will be published inside the company. You can read more about that in a company's news flash tomorrow, but I though you'd love to hear it from me already today."

The whole auditorium applauded, and even Martin, who felt torn apart between understanding that certain changes were necessary and uncertainty about what that all would mean for him, clapped his hands.

"Furthermore," Mr. Kennedy interrupted his thoughts, "I'm very proud of another great catch. I'd like to introduce you to our new Chief People & Ethics Officer, Dr. Selma Adams. She's a member of our Executive Committee, because a people expert in the top team is most vital for our new approach."

The people who were sitting in front of Martin stood up to catch a glimpse of her so that he couldn't see anything for a few moments before he himself rose as well.

"Selma Adams, as it turns out, has a German dad and a Japanese mum. That's why she also speaks Japanese, which I will never learn, but she said that's OK with her." He pretended to wipe sweat from his forehead with one hand and throw it to the floor in relief. The whole auditorium laughed at his joke.

"Selma studied business administration at Stanford University and obtained her doctor's degree with summa cum laude in philosophy at the University of Heidelberg. Selma has held corporate human resources positions with industrial companies in Germany, Singapore and India. She also holds an additional degree in ethics, which you'll find to be very pleasant when she walks her talk. And which makes me feel severely undereducated if you know what I mean." He grinned as if he had revealed a secret he was not allowed to tell and again had all laughs on his side.

"Selma will also be in charge of monitoring and reporting on how good we are in curing our sick behavioral patterns. Plus she needs to broaden our recruiting approach for leaders to include screening a person's character. She'll report to the CEO and also be in contact with the Chairwoman of the Ethics Committee on a regular basis. Would you please welcome Selma Adams!" He motioned for Selma to join him on stage and say a few words. The people in the auditorium stretched their necks to have a good look at her. Most welcomed her with a short applause.

Martin watched the woman stand up and walk towards Mr. Kennedy gracefully. She was petite but even from that distance she had an aura of firm softness no woman Martin had ever encountered had had. She wore a dark blue pantsuit and a white silk blouse that fell softly around her neck. But she sent a fashion statement with plain-brogue double monk shoes in red and pink leather and a matching red lipstick that enhanced her slightly Asian features framed by long black hair. Martin's lips parted. He touched his mouth with his fingers and his pupils widened. His imagination began to run wild.

"Good morning, colleagues," Selma opened in a firm voice and with sparkling eyes. "I have joined this company because with my mind, heart and soul I believe in the path chosen by the main shareholders. To me it is a most sensible approach in today's world. My descent, my upbringing, my education and most of all my children taught me that everything is interconnected in our world today. What unites us is the fact that we are human beings and equal by essence. We all strive for a better world, and in that we're also moral creatures. That to me stands paramount."

She was interrupted by warm applause.

"What makes us different from each other is merely the pool of abilities and views that together hold the potential of all humanity. And we in the chemical industry hold the key to the well-being of many of our fellow men, women, children and our planet. Let's use all our abilities."

Many people once again clapped their hands and looked at each other in excitement.

"Who I am and what I stand for is best expressed through my daily work. And I say this for me and for you. It is by our example, by our behavior that we set the tone and pace for the future of our company. If we don't care about our morals expressed in our four values, why should anyone else in this company care? Ethics and morals seem to be 'in' right now, sexy buzzwords, good for PR campaigns and employer branding. But I tell you these are not just sexy words to play around with. There are strongly committed shareholders, who pay for an independent and scientifically sound Ethics Committee, behind all of this. This is not a nice-to-have working party. Nor is it a fig leaf for the Board or ExCom. The Ethics Committee will provide decision makers with unbiased moral opinions based on our four values, human rights and international standards in Corporate Social Responsibility. This is what we commit to as leaders and also as a company."

"But who committed us to the morality of the four values?" Martin called from the last row, his eyes fixed on Selma. He felt an inner urge to get noticed by her. People turned around and looked at him.

"Brilliant question, thank you," Selma replied with a smile. "The answer is: You did!"

Martin and many others stretched their necks and stared at her.

"That's right, you did. The morality of our four values has been part of the company for ages. When you signed your employment contract, you agreed to them, at least implicitly by accepting the handout about the values that you received with the contract. When you signed the contract, you were aware that you joined an ethical company. The fact that your experience in the company has been a different one is mainly because our guiding values have degenerated to a marketing tool."

Martin swallowed, and so did many others in the room while a few people were applauding her, among them George and Mr. Kennedy.

"But I have a lot of hope," Selma continued, "especially in the younger generation. They make us look at our values and live them because they pick or leave their employer based on company values and how they are applied. They point their fingers at those greedy managers who feel free from any moral limitations if it comes to their personal interests."

Martin felt excited and shaken up by her at the same time. "I can't believe it," he kept repeating, holding the sides of his head.

"You can make up your mind about me when we collaborate with each other," she continued. "However, there's one thing I want you to know right now. When I work, I give it my all for the benefit of the vision and the mission that need to be realized. But I'm also a single mum, and when one of my three daughters, Ashmita, Bethari or Charlotte, needs me, I will drop everything, and I ask you to respect that. I look forward to working with you. Thank you."

She received an enthusiastic applause from the females and some men in the room. Martin's eyes started to gloss over, and his muscles relaxed a bit. A slow smile started to spread over his face. A pleasant shiver went through his body, which was still sweaty and tense. What a woman, he thought when she left the stage and Mr. Kennedy took over again.

"Ladies and gentlemen, 'it's tea time', as we say in Ireland. There's tea and coffee with snacks for all of us in the lounge outside. And if you give me the pleasure of talking to me about your thoughts and worries, I'll add one of my lemon sherbet sweets."

He smiled and motioned the audience to follow him outside to the lounge area.

CHAPTER 4

Franz Winter spotted Martin, who was getting himself an espresso, and walked right over to him. Wrinkling his nose, Martin tried to avert his gaze and escape him, but he couldn't manage because others stood in his way to collect their coffee. Franz Winter had been Chairman of the Works Council for seven years now and was already campaigning for his re-election next year. His deputy, Mr. Ralph Lorenz, was right on his heals for this influential position. Martin disliked Franz Winter. Winter reminded him of his father, an officer of the British Royal Forces, and how miserable he had made Martin's childhood. Franz Winter was equally fanatic about the military and the means he employed to achieve his goals were just as clever. He constantly bragged about being an excellent paintball player, and nobody, including Martin, believed him because he was in his late fifties, short and stocky. With his chubby face, blue eyes and rimless glasses, his high forehead and grey beard Franz Winter looked like a teddy bear when he smiled but like a demon when his face was grim.

Mr. Winter dragged Martin away from the coffee counter. "What're you making of all of this, Dr. Fox?" He leaned towards Martin as if to conspire.

"Have you been at the CEO's address as well?"

"Of course. I wasn't invited but I need to be informed, if you know what I mean." He winked at Martin.

"I don't quite see where it's going yet, Mr. Winter," Martin replied cautiously so as not to disclose what he really thought.

"If Bergan and Kennedy succeed with their plans, Dr. Fox, we

Germans will loose everything, everything, I'm telling you. Your and my influence will be gone. But I'll stop Bergan. Oh yes, I will. You can count on me." Franz Winter opened his right hand with its sausage-like fingers and a signet ring as if he were holding George Bergan in his palm before he clenched it to a fist. A shudder went through Martin's whole body.

"How do you intend to do that, if I may ask?" Curiously, Martin leaned towards Mr. Winter.

Winter whispered, "Everybody has a past. And I'll make that Dr. Bergan stumble over his past. Just listen to the news on the radio tomorrow."

Before Martin could react, Peter Stark, the CFO, and Karl Kirch joined them with coffee. Both were on good speaking terms with Franz Winter. Martin, by contrast, perceived Karl Kirch to be his fiercest rival for an ExCom position and the CFO he didn't trust at all. Peter Stark's nickname in the company was 'The First Bodyguard of Capital'. He knew his numbers inside out but didn't let anyone else understand them equally well. Martin recalled that Karin had said that Mr. Stark resembled a table lamp with its ceremonial seriousness. And when he looked at him right now standing there stiff and petrified, her description indeed hit it on the nail. Peter Stark radiated a kind of deliberation as if he were carrying the risk of always threatened financial stocks on his shoulders. He had a bullish appearance, an almost bald cube-shaped head and thick lips. Martin considered him to be extremely ugly. Concern, not wisdom seemed to live behind his notched forehead. Martin liked to tease him about that.

"What do you think about all of that, my friend?" Franz Winter asked. "Do you agree with me that Bergan and Kennedy must be stopped?"

"We'll be the laughing stock of the stock exchange if they succeed," Stark replied in an ascetic tone while his fingers turned claw-like and his nostrils flared.

"And what do you make of your new colleague in the ExCom, this Selma Adams?" Frank Winter's mouth quivered.

"Women don't belong on the battle field. That's my opinion," Peter Stark replied curtly.

"That's exactly what I say. Put them in the kitchen and let them raise the kids."

Martin had the smile of a connoisseur on his face while wondering if this gorgeous beauty was wearing a sexy lace teddy underneath and whom she would allow to help her out of it?

CHAPTER 5

It was 8.20 pm. The air in hotel room was sticky with a mixture of sweat and her perfume, a spicy oriental fragrance with notes of pink pepper, Turkish rose, raspberry blossoms, papyrus and white amber. Martin was lying naked on his back, staring at the cream-colored stucco ceiling, the white starched cotton bedclothes pushed down to his hips. She slipped out of the bed, collected her lingerie from the floor and went into the bathroom. After a few moments, Martin could hear the shower at work. He felt numb and empty. He had just had sex with a woman he hardly even knew by name. She had a smooth belly and large breasts and had felt like an over-ripe rose-petal. She was the type of woman he preferred: well-off but lonely career women he could casually pick up after meetings with banks, law firms, and consultancies. Time and time again, he needed that. He wasn't able to stop it.

Everyone of them he had had sex with had only made his loneliness worse. Still staring at the ceiling, he suddenly realized that this was not the right cure for him. He had always been a womanizer, true. To him, love was a dunghill and he was the cock on top of it, crowing, ruffling his feathers. He was used to slipping into familiar lies. How could a woman know that he meant none of what he said, that he merely spoke from habit, from the urge to get them into bed just once or twice, only pretending intimacy whilst avoiding it like a plague?

She came back into the room in sexy red lingerie, a detail Martin had not noticed until now. She slipped into her black sheath dress and matching high heals, put on her luxury earrings, watch and bracelet. She moved over to the couch table, took her smart-phone out of her huge black designer handbag and started to text someone while the corners of her mouth went up. She was pleased about something but it couldn't be him. She put the smartphone back into her bag and wrapped herself in a pashmina that had a pastel shade of violet, shutting herself off from him and what had just happened. She walked towards the door with rigor. Before opening it, she turned around to Martin.

"I think that's it."

"Yes," Martin said, adding absent-mindedly, "What's the name of your perfume?"

"Rose of No Man's Land," She replied with a tear in her eye.

That's how the nurses were called who cared for the wounded soldiers between the trenches in World War I, Martin remembered, brooding.

"You know what? Where other men have a heart, you have a stone. And as long as you don't get rid of it, you'll never find what you're looking for."

"What do you think I am looking for?" Martin growled, clenching his teeth while his stomach revolted.

"Love, unconditional love," her sulky lips fired at him before she walked out the door and slammed it shut.

Martin picked up his smartphone from the carpet at his bedside and texted to Karl Kirch: "Just had the Strategy Consultant PZ as well. Add two points to my score. Guess I'm in the lead, right?"

It was only seconds before Martin heard a bling bling. He gazed at the display. "Fuck you!"

That brought a smile to his face.

How long it eventually took him to get up and go into the bathroom, he didn't know. He stood naked in front of the huge mirror for several minutes, looking at himself appraisingly from head to toe. The beginning of a pot belly, declining muscles that felt stiff and tense, deep wrinkles around his eyes, varicose veins, and more grey hair than ever before on his head and chest. Where had the tall and slender guy gone who had once been a Bavarian fencing champion? The one with a healthy sun tan and sandy blond hair? The one who had moved swiftly and gracefully, with well-trained muscles, flexible ligaments and tendons? Out of nowhere he shouted at himself, "I hate what has become of you – you despicable bastard!" Instantly, he felt a cramping pain in his stomach and broke out in sweat from head to toe. Finally Martin stepped into the shower.

CHAPTER 6

"I'm home. Helen, where are you?" Martin called out.

He left the foyer in search of her, noticing a large oil painting in bubble wrap on his way to the kitchen. He went to the fridge for a bottle of beer, opened it with a loud plop, picked a glass from the cupboard, poured the beer and gulped it down so thirstily as if he had had to do without anything liquid all day.

"Oh, so here you are, darling." He discovered her sitting in one of the two Eames chairs under the light of his beloved Achille Castiglioni arch-lamp in front of the huge window overlooking their garden that extended into the valley and gave a view of the skyline of Frankfurt. She sat there with her sketchbook on her lap and had evidently just begun to draw a scene from memory – a man and a woman in a sailing boot, who tenderly gazed at each other. A jar with some hundred coloured pencils sat next to her on the adjustable Eileen Green side-table in between the two chairs. He looked at her. Something about her was different. Had she had her hair cut today? That reminded him of this morning. He had forgotten to text her to apologize. It didn't seem to have upset her anyway. He dropped into the empty chair beside her and emptied his beer glass in one gulp.

"Let me guess, darling," he said eventually, "you've painted another picture and at long last sold one, right? I noticed it in the hallway."

"Not yet, but I might sell it. It'll be picked up by a gallery employee for an exposition Anna and I do together in downtown Frankfurt starting next Wednesday."

"Your painter friend from Art School – must've been ages since I last saw her."

"You're welcome to join the vernissage with drinks and speeches at 7 pm."

Martin's mind had already wandered off to music. His eyes started to search for the remote control when Helen intervened sharply.

"I need to talk to you, right now and seriously." She said it as if she was announcing a solar eclipse.

"Do you want help in the household to give you more time to paint?"

"Try to listen, Martin, will you?"

He abandoned the thought of music and put the beer glass down on the wooden floor.

"What is it then?"

"I've signed a power of attorney with a lawyer to file for divorce and, if necessary, to represent me in any settlement negotiation with you inside or outside of court."

Martin's face petrified in pain as if someone had just dumped a bucket of ice water on his head. When the first shiver was gone, he replied, "That's a joke, right?" But he instantly knew that she wasn't joking. She never did about those kinds of things.

"This a not a marriage based on mutual love, let alone care or even respect any more," she said harshly while getting up. Her eyes were cold and flinty now. "Christopher, the successful medical student, and I, the cute little housewife with the amusing quirk of painting oil canvases of people in need – we just provide the cover image for your career and a place to rest your feet and laptop from time to time."

Martin swallowed. His face turned red while his stomach revolted again.

"You're over-dramatizing. It's true, I haven't been home very often. But I did that all for you. The house, our comfortable lifestyle –"

"No, Martin. You did that all for yourself, just yourself and nobody else. We were just extras in a film called Martin the Great."

"I know what it is." Martin had a suspicion. "It's another man, right?"

"Well yes, there has been another man in my life ... for about a year now."

"What kind of bullshit is that?" he shouted. With his left hand he wiped the jar with pencils off the table. The pencils scattered all over the floor. He jumped to his feet and towered over her, grabbing her by the shoulders as if he could control her that way.

"Helen," he said, shaking her, "come to your senses! Everything's fine. OK, you have an affair, so what? And I work too much, so what?"

Disgusted, she pushed him away with all her strength. "Why don't you talk about all the affairs you pretend never happened and still are happening?"

Martin's eyes narrowed. He felt caught. Did she know? How much did she know?

"But didn't we have a good time together? Didn't we start out really well?" Martin asked, trying to turn the conversation around in his favour.

Helen reminisced. "When we were students, we had little money but we had dreams and ideals. We went on your first adventure to Africa together, on a shoestring, and were overwhelmed by the beauty and wilderness of its nature as well as by the misery of its people. On the veranda of a tiny lodge at Etosha National Park overlooking the lake you asked me if I would move to Africa with you if you'd build a company that helped to purify water so that more people could have access to clean and healthy water all year. I said, 'If you do that, I'll follow you, no matter what kind of life we'll have.' And when we got back to Munich I discovered that I was pregnant."

"Yes," Martin said, flinching slightly.

"After your graduation, you wanted to gain some three to five years of experience first. With the help of your professor you landed the job as Assistant to the CEO in this company. But with every year the dream of going to Africa and working on something that mattered to your chemist's heart faded away a bit more. Part of who you were and what I loved so much about you died many years ago –"

"No, Helen, that's not right," he insisted.

"I can show you by just reflecting on our wedding anniversaries."

"What do they have to do with it?"

"It would be nice of you to just listen carefully. Maybe then you'll get the message." Helen's muscles started to quiver, her pulse sped up and her heart pounded. Time to let it all out. "During the first three years, we took a day off to celebrate being together by exploring something new. Then you went on for five years to work as a controller in one of the German subsidiaries close by. In these years you took me out to dinner to fancy restaurants. First you picked me up at home with a beautiful bouquet of flowers in my favourite colours. You dressed up, too, and off we went for a wonderful evening filled with fun and laughter. In your last year in this position you had me come to the restaurant on my own. You were late for dinner some forty-five minutes and twice on the phone with some colleague of yours during the main course and the dessert."

"Helen, wait – that's beyond the point."

"For once just listen to me, Martin!" It had never happened before that Helen insisted that he should listen to her. "Our tenth anniversary you just forgot. You gave me a diamond ring a week later, though I thought you knew that I dislike diamonds. During the next couple of years as a Team Leader Business Development you mostly travelled and gave me a gift on your return, a scarf, a purse or earrings. No time together any more. You bought these impersonal gifts at some airport luxury shop you passed by on your way home."

"How do you know that?"

"I found the receipts of the purchases in the pockets of your jackets when I emptied them before I took them to the dry-cleaner."

Martin swallowed in acknowledgement.

"During the five years that we lived in Antwerp while you were in charge of the Belgian subsidiary, I had to join you for business dinners and receptions on our special day. You always said that you needed to prove that you would do as well as a manager with a line management career path."

"Of course I had to, but you never understood that. Admit it, you had a great time in Antwerp studying the Flemish Masters, Rubens, Anthony Van Dyck –, " he said defensively.

"Shut up, Martin, shut up and listen."

He hid his hands in his pockets.

"Once you were promoted to Head of Corporate Development, it became even worse. You not only travelled most of the time, you also got an MBA in the U.S. In those years our wedding anniversary was reduced to cards with a few words of affection. At our last anniversary, the card arrived via your secretary, who had signed it on your behalf. Is it funny or is it humiliating to receive a wedding anniversary card saying 'I love you' signed by your husband's secretary? You tell me."

Martin was silent, breathing heavily. Then he recollected

himself, pulled his hands up, ready to defend what he had and desperately wanted to keep. "Its bullshit to narrow the bad experiences in our marriage down to the fun days we've missed. Get real, Helen!"

"OK. You want the other side? You can have that as well. Where were you when Christopher had his first day in school? Where were you to support Christopher and me in the first few days after he had his snowboard accident and had to be brought into intensive care by helicopter?"

"But I gave a speech at Christopher's graduation from school."

"Where were you to support me when my parents died in a car crash at the Amalfi coast?" Tears were streaming down her cheeks and a hot wave flushed her body.

"But what difference would it have made if I helped you fill in Italian paperwork and arrange for the transfer of their corpses to Munich?"

Helen swallowed, and her tears ran down her face like two rivers. "That's something only somebody who suffers from social-emotional autism could ask. You know, Christopher and I have given up on the hope that you will ever realise what's going with the people around you and what they truly need."

Martin bent forward and buried his head in his hands, eager to strike back but not knowing how for the moment.

Helen blew her nose and said in a carefully controlled voice, "I will move to Hamburg at the end of this month at the latest so I can be with Alexander."

Martin's face clouded over with sadness. He felt a headache hammering in his head. "Who is he? I demand to know."

Helen looked at the deep dark valley and the illuminated skyline of Frankfurt in the distance, crossing her arms in front of her chest. "There's nothing you can demand any more."

"I won't grant you a divorce. Never. And if you want alimony, you'll need to fight for it." Martin didn´t dare to look at her. His cheeks started to burn, and he could feel his pulse hammering in his throat.

Helen, by contrast, calmed down even more. She felt confident that she would win this battle sooner rather than later. After all, she had Alexander and Anna at her side to protect her if needed. She turned around and stepped towards him, taking his head into her hands to force him to look at her. "For two-and-a-half decades, I confined myself to be a kind caretaker of your needs. I suppressed my own needs and went wherever you wanted me to go, doing whatever you wanted me to do, nearly destroying my talent by letting it stay dormant. Not for one day longer will I ignore my own needs and support your selfishness that way." Abruptly, she pushed his face away and walked towards the staircase. "I've put bed linen into the guest room. The lawyer advised me to start the clock of separation ticking as of tonight."

After she had left, Martin bent down and fell to his knees. With wet eyes he tried to pick up the colour pencils and put them back into the jar. His hands trembled. He couldn't manage to pick up any of them.

CHAPTER 7

"Thank you, Hans, for coming over before your surgery opens," Helen said as she opened the front door. "You'll find him in the guestroom. I've put cold wraps around his calves as a first remedy to bring the fever down some thirty minutes ago."

"40° Celsius is not nothing. When did it start?"

"After we had an argument last night, I guess."

"Helen, are you OK?"

"Please just take over – as a doctor and as his friend. Can you do that for me?"

Hans wasn't quite sure what she was hinting at, but he appreciated Helen so much that he would have said 'yes' to anything before he knew what it was. He kissed her on both cheeks.

"Don't worry, I will. By the way thanks for the invitation. Looking forward to a night out with artists."

"I'm very nervous about this. Anna is an accomplished and celebrated artist. I'm just her friend from Art School."

"If necessary, I'll hold your hand."

"There's already someone else who takes care of that. But you'll enjoy seeing Christopher. He's coming all the way form Berlin just to support me that evening."

Hans smiled in anticipation. He wouldn't do that for his father, he thought while walking up the staircase to the guestroom.

"I didn't expect to see you again this week," Hans said quietly after he had slowly entered the guestroom.

Martin turned around in his single bed that stood along the wall across from of the door and looked at Hans. His face was glowing. His eyes were pale and watery. Two pages with notes were scattered in front of his bed, crumpled and wet. Hans picked them up and smoothened the pages before putting them aside so that he could sit on the edge of Martin's bed. He took Martin's temperature – 39.9° C – and shook his head. Then he checked his pulse, blood pressure, throat, eyes and lungs before taking a blood sample.

"What is it?" Martin asked anxiously, his eyes blinking infrequently.

"It looks like a small system breakdown."

Martin remained silent.

"Did somebody kick your butt?"

"Not funny. My world is collapsing and I don't know how to fight it."

"Fight whom or what?"

"Helen, her lover, George, everybody and everything –"

"For the next weeks, surely not."

Hans picked up the papers again to take a closer look at them. Martin turned around to face the wall while pondering how best to kill himself. A grand finale of putting the blame on others might be a solution. Hans started to read out loud: Five Clusters of Sick

Leadership Behaviours in our Company (by George Bergan, CEO, 7th of May 2015)

The Egocentrics are lordly-type leaders who perceive themselves as "immune", "indispensable", "superior" or even "immortal". They are ambitious and boastful, defining their place in the world through outer appearances. The clothes they wear as well as the symbols and medals of honour they received have been gained through rivalry and struggle. They aspire power, positions, profits and perks. They put themselves on display. To stand out as more capable than others, they may use any means.

The Workaholics are leaders who are constantly busy and so neglect themselves in body, mind and soul as well as their loved ones, their friends, their co-workers and others. There is no time for regular self-reflection. They are closed to all that is lively, fresh, imaginative and new because they only work according to their established ideas and plans, thereby missing what is real right now. They are keen on taming life according to their ideas. They have lost contact and with it the fluent interaction with the community around them, pretending that they don't need others to go about their work.

The Heart-of-Stone Guys are leaders who are intellectually and spiritually petrified. They have degenerated to paper pushers and sometimes resemble a machine more than a human being. Their human sensitivity is gone. They only think about themselves. They lack honesty and warmth in human relations. They don't share their knowledge and expertise with others for the purpose of the common good. Out of envy or slyness they take joy in the mistakes and misfortunes of others. They believe that being serious about something requires gloomy, severe faces, instead of spreading joy and friendliness. They shine by behaving strict, hard and arrogant towards anyone they consider lower in rank. They paper over the emptiness in their hearts by filling their lives with money as well as things they do not need but which give them a feeling of security. They have lost the understanding of what is enough for them and what others may legitimately ask for.

"Shut up," Martin mumbled. He rolled back on his back and started to hammer his fists into the mattress.

"Fine, but permit me to finish reading, will you?"

"Do what you have to do."

Hans continued silently.

The Self-Forgotten are leaders who are chronically forgetful about being a child of God, unable to express the God-like qualities of love and caring for the whole. Their spiritual emptiness is covered up with diplomas and academic achievements. Many lead a double life, preaching water to others while they drink wine.

The Masked are leaders who gossip, grumble and backbite whilst showing a polished and polite mask to those they harm with their words. To smoothen their way to the top they echo what their superiors say and glorify them. They have a tendency to live in cliques that deliberately close themselves off from the company at large.

"Great stuff Martin. I give you four and a half out of five. What score did your boss give you?"

"And I thought you were my friend," Martin grumbled barely audibly, gritting his teeth.

"I have been since we shared a room in boarding school and had our first secret cigarette in the boys' room together. By the way, did you take the pills I prescribed to you Monday?"

"No."

"Great, Mr. Invincible doesn't need medical support. Then I'll go back to the patients who take my prescriptions seriously."

Hans closed his doctor's bag made of seasoned brown leather and was about to leave the room when Martin turned towards him. In tears and with a whiney voice he said, "Don't go! If you leave me, I'm all alone."

"Where has Martin gone?" Hans turned around, moved back to his bed and sat down at his side. "The one who helped shy Hans get his first girl friend? For several years I've only seen a lousy copy of this cold-hearted British Army officer, Colonel Lenard Fox, who happened to be your begetter."

Martin swallowed. Tears ran down his face.

"You mean the Martin who stood by you when your father yelled at you to 'cut your hair and learn something decent'?"

"The one who went out of his way to be by my side whenever I needed support in daring to do something for the first time."

"Like playing your trumpet in front of an audience."

Hans nodded silently.

"Martin has become a successful manager just short of the move into the ExCom," he said, looking at Hans with a contemptuous glance. "And you – look at you. All you've become is a local M.D. with a boring life. You never get around, always sleep with one and the same woman. I don't know why you're still my friend?"

"Your wickedness has feathers today. Barely able to stand on his feet, but piteous as an old vulture."

Martin scrubbed a hand over his sweaty red-hot face. "Sorry, Hans. You're the only one who really knows me and still hasn't turned around and walked away."

"I still believe in the good inside of you that you've hidden away for some time now. But make it easier on me in the second part of our life, will you?"

Martin remained silent and stared at the ceiling.

"Don't you get it, Hans? I'm close to total defeat."

"All you are is sick in bed with fever."

"I might not make it to the ExCom."

"It's not the end of the world if you don't get your wish list ticked."

Martin shook his head. "Yes, it is, but you don't get that."

"Who knows?"

Martin' eyes blinked infrequently. He was dead tired.

"I'll be back tomorrow, Martin. Pack some T-shirts, jeans and a pullover. I'll take you with me then, provided you take the pills on the table, two each three times a day, and drink lots of water. Ask Helen to continue with the cold wraps and prepare some fresh chicken soup for you."

"She doesn't care for my demands any longer," Martin replied, barely audible.

"That might be a very clever decision –"

Hans went downstairs and handed the sick slip for the company to Helen.

"He'll be out of the rat race for ten to fourteen days. Anything I need to know from your side, Helen?"

"I hired a lawyer to file for divorce yesterday. I told him late last night when he came home. I'm about to pack my bags and leave for Hamburg."

"Does my godson already know about this development?"

"I'll call Christopher later today to let him know what happened."

"Is their father-son relationship still as tense as it used to be?"

"No improvement since Martin threw a painting of Christopher's into the bin right in front of his eyes with the words 'and what's that supposed to be?"

"He was just four years old –" Hans felt s sharp pain in his chest saying it.

"Martin has kept adding emotional scars to him and me ever since." Helen's eyes became wet.

Hmmmm. Hans exhaled deeply and sniffled. "Tell Christopher I love you all and that he should give me a call."

"Thank you, Hans."

"I'll be back tomorrow and if Martin is able to get up again, I'll take him with me."

"Won't that be too big a burden on you and May May?"

"She's in Shanghai for a Traditional Chinese Medicine conference and to spend some time with her family. She'll be gone for a month. With Martin in the house, I might not feel quite as lonely."

"Thanks so much, Hans," She said, lifting her head as if she was sending her gratitude to heaven.

"Forgive him, Helen. He's blind, unable to see the gems he's holding in the palm of his hands while searching the world for something else."

They hugged each other and Hans kissed her good-bye on the cheek.

CHAPTER 8

Martin sat at Hans's round wooden kitchen table, enjoying a freshly brewed espresso coffee. It was Monday morning around 10 am. Martin had slept nearly all weekend and felt a lot better. He was setting his sights again on how to become a member of the ExCom now. Hans returned from his adjacent surgery, dressed in his doctor's coat, and entered the kitchen with some lab results in his hands. To Martin's surprise he was not in his usual joking mode but had a severe look on his face. Hans sat down facing Martin and looked straight at him. Martin pulled his mouth into a straight line and bit his lips while tugging his pullover into a more proper fit. He had a strange feeling that he wouldn't like what was to come now.

"Martin," Hans said with serious concern in his voice, "your medical condition is a lot more serious than just high blood pressure, reflux and a cholesterol level that is too high."

Martin got up, put his espresso cup under the coffee machine and pressed the button while rubbing his face in worry. He returned to the table with the refilled espresso cup in his right hand while biting the nails of his left hand. He barely looked at Hans. "What do you mean? The fever is gone. Nothing hurts any more."

"Martin, if you continue to live and work like you did the last couple of years, you're on your way to early retirement, either due to a stroke or a heart attack. And down that line even kidney failure is possible. If you decide to tackle what is out of balance now, it will take some months to a year to get you in shape again – provided you change your way of going about your work as well. I will provide you with medication for this transformation period. That's the news I have for you as your doctor."

Martin put his cup down and looked at the floor. After a few moments he said almost inaudibly, "That can't be."

"I'm sorry, Martin, but that's the way it is," Hans replied firmly.

"Are you telling me I should give up my career ambitions and become one of these unrecognizable grey mice on the lower floors that go home early?"

"All I'm saying is that I strongly recommend that you seriously review all aspects of your life and dare to make changes or there might not be much fun left for you sooner rather than later."

"But isn't there an alternative solution? Couldn't you just provide me with medication and I just continue the way I did?"

"I had a guy like you just forty-six years of age in my surgery last month telling me the same."

"So?"

"He is dead now. Didn't survive his first heart attack a week ago."

Hans pushed the lap report across the table. Martin saw that three parameters had been marked in deep red and one had been circled with a large question mark next to it.

"Have you taken any substance lately to enhance your performance?"

Embarrassed, Martin looked down again. "Yes, I have," he whispered.

"For how long, Martin?"

"When George took office, I saw my chance. I felt and looked tired too often. I couldn't sleep well for the last couple of years. If I wanted to be ahead of my potential competitors for an ExCom position, I knew that I needed to push myself to the limit, looking fresh and radiant. In the evenings I drank more than I used to so I would be able to sleep, and to relax, I had sex with lonely career women who were available for a night or two."

"Did it ever occur to you that showing weakness is very human and that it could also be a selection criterion to behave human?"

"Not in the shark ponds where I'm earning my money and stripes."

Hans shook his head. "Have you ever considered that you were not born the way you behave now?"

Martin shrugged. He drew his head into his shoulders. His face froze and his body stiffened.

Hans got up and placed himself right in front of Martin. "This was my statement as your doctor. Now here is what I have to tell you as your one and only friend."

Martin remained silent, looking up at Hans.

"I've booked you an appointment with Rupert Hess at 3 pm. He's one of the finest body-mind-soul therapists I know. I want you to listen to what he has to tell you."

CHAPTER 9

"Hello, Karin, it's me." Martin switched his smartphone from his right to his left ear. "Just wanted to check how things are going at the office."

"Good morning, Dr. Fox. Hope you feel better after a long weekend's rest."

"Well, yes, thank you. Must have caught some virus. It'll take a few more days before I'm my old self again, the doctor said thirty minutes ago."

"Well, that's great news."

"Karin, I'd like to stay on top of things. Can you give me a quick overview of my mails? Just the most important things that are going on."

"The things that are really of interest to you aren't in your mail box, I guess."

"Karin, stop teasing me. What is it?" Martin switched his smart phone to his right ear again.

"Where do you want me to start?"

"Are there any really good news? I could do with some..."

"The Head of Business Unit Performance Products has been released from his position with immediate effect."

"Yay!" Martin slapped himself on his thigh, grinning widely. "How the hell did that happen?"

"Well, the Chairman and George constantly repeated that our values are non-negotiable and Respect is one of them, gell?"

"So?"

"As the story goes, last Friday morning around 10 am this very gentleman had entered the lift at bistro level to go up when Branka Horvat followed him with the food and beverages service trolley for the Executive floor. He pushed her and the trolley back out, saying for many others to overhear, 'I don't share the lift with service personnel.' And tough luck for him, one of those who saw and heard it was George himself. Half an hour later he was asked to come to the CEO's office. The rest you can imagine, can't you?"

Martin remained silent.

"Nobody really likes him, right? He finally got what he deserved if you ask me."

"Karin, you made my day … yay!" Martin got up and pretended to fence an imaginative opponent, striking the deadly blow.

"Not so fast – it get's even better, Dr. Fox."

"What can be sweeter than that, Karin?"

"What people liked even more is what happened afterwards. Branka was called to George's office where he officially apologized to her and handed her a huge bouquet of tulips in all colours. He told her how much he appreciated her dedication to her work and how service-minded she does it with a smile on her face every day, no matter what. The people at the low end of the hierarchy are over the moon. Our company is no longer applying two sets of rules, one for the bosses and one for the ordinary people."

Martin's eyes widened. He means it, he thought, George really means it.

"But there are two really irritating incidents as well," she said in a disturbed voice that he knew only too well. Karin believed in the good of people, and every time this belief was shaken, the pitch of her voice became higher.

"Karin, calm down. What is it?"

"You didn't follow the news, did you? Otherwise you'd already know."

The news? No, he didn't. He had either been too weak and sleepy or he had enjoyed his time with Hans, watching the old Star Wars movies in anticipation of the new one to be released by the end of the year. Or, even more fun, they had been playing car crash video games.

"A local radio station reported on Friday it had written evidence that Dr. George Bergan is HIV positive. And that this was most likely due to him being bi-sexual, which started during some wild years in New York. The radio said that they had asked for his comment but that Dr. Bergan was not available for that. On the other hand the Chairman of the Works Council was interviewed. And he said that if this was true, it would be wise if Dr. Bergan stepped down to protect the reputation of the company. The newspapers are full of it today."

Martin took a deep breath and touched his throat.

"Do you think it's true, Dr. Fox?"

"I can't think at all now, Karin," He said while his eyes blinked rapidly.

"I can't believe it, Dr. Fox. Neither can many others. But Mr. Winter assured us that the evidence it convincing. We don't want this to be true. We want him to be healthy, and we want him to stay."

"I know, Karin."

He could tell that Karin was in tears. She blew her nose and continued in a whiney voice, "I haven't finished yet. Friday evening, the police simultaneously searched the office of our Chief Financial Officer and his home. Apparently Peter Stark's name is on a CD that the government acquired from Switzerland with names of tax evaders. The outcome of that is still unknown, but Peter Stark has not shown up today."

Martin raised his eyebrows and felt his heartbeat picking up. What would that all mean for him? "Karin, I have to digest this. I'll be back. Thank you."

CHAPTER 10

Life is Movement – Rupert Hess – Osteopath – Bioenergetics Therapist – Meditation Master, the sign read. Martin rang the doorbell. He waited on the doorstep with his arms crossed, not really interested in what this guy might have to say. A young man dressed in white opened the door, took his jacket and asked him to take off his shoes before entering the therapy room. "I'll inform Mr. Hess that you're here," he said and disappeared. The room was some forty square meters in size. It was flooded with warm sunlight, and its huge windows looked over a Japanese-style garden. The room had a light-coloured wooden floor, eggshell-coloured walls with a fair amount of water paintings, sketches of fluid body movements of both, men and women. It was furnished with two comfortable armchairs in terracotta-brown leather, which were placed near the windows, a small music system, two meditation cushions, two yoga mats and a singing bowl.

"Nice to meet you. My name's Rupert Hess," said a man who looked like he was in his mid-fifties and offered Martin his hand. Martin appraised him from head to toe. Hess was about his own height; he had well-trimmed grey hair, warm hands and radiant eyes. His body was slim, his movements fluid and easy. He wore white doctors' trousers with a light brown cotton belt, a light blue shirt with rolled-up sleeves but neither shoes nor socks. There was something about him that made Martin feel comfortable though he couldn't tell what it was.

"Martin Fox, pleased to meet you."

"Come on, let's sit over there," Rupert Hess said, pointing to the two chairs by the window.

"So what brought you to me, Mr. Fox?", he asked after they had settled down.

"My friend, Doctor Hans Jacobi, made this appointment for me. He thought it might be a good idea if you'd have a look at me as well."

"And you've come to please him, but not because you think this is a good idea?"

Martin started fidgeting. "To be honest – yes."

"Then why should I waste my time with you?"

Martin cleared this throat. "Because I pay you for doing that?"

"I don't need your money, Mr. Fox. I work with people who are ready to make the most of their lives. That is what motivates me to work with someone."

"I want to make the most of my life, too."

"Really?" Rupert Hess challenged him. "Tell me."

"I'm forty-eight and have never been seriously sick in my life, but I haven't been well lately. My work has started to take its toll on my body."

"What kind of work do you do?"

"I'm a top manager with a global responsibility in a major international industrial company."

"That includes a lot of air travel, long hours sitting in air conditioned buildings, quite a few business dinners, little to no sports and relaxation, very limited time with your family and friends. Would that about sum it up?"

“Very much so, Mr. Hess.” Martin nodded so pointedly that even his torso slightly moved back and forth.

“So what are your ambitions?”

“I love to decide and shape thing according to my views. My next career goal is to become a member of the Executive Committee of our company. That’s where the real decisions are made.”

“Do you have guts, Mr. Fox?”

“Do I look like a wimp to you?”

“Looks don’t matter, deeds count.”

Martin got up. “I accept your challenge.”

“Good. Then take off your socks and your pullover, stand up and follow me to the mirror over there.”

Martin did as he was told. In small, jerky steps he walked behind Mr. Hess. Breathing faster, he positioned himself in front of the mirror. He felt a slight chill going through his body and rubbed his forearms before he lowered them.

“Please relax and then describe to me what you’re seeing and feeling, Mr. Fox.”

Martin tensely looked at himself in the mirror. He had no idea how long it took for him to reply. “My face looks impenetrable. My eyes are empty. My skin is pale. My hands and feet are cold, very cold. I draw in my head. My shoulders look like a coat hanger. My neck is stiff and hurts, as it does most of the time. My jawbones feel tense, as they are most of the time. The upper half of my body looks oversized in relation to the lower half. My whole body feels stiff, and my lower spine hurts.”

“Tell me how your feet feel the ground, Mr. Fox.”

Martin rolled his feet from toes to heels a couple of times.

“Do you feel the warmth of the wood under your feet or are

you just mechanically in touch with it?"

"I don't know. I really can't tell you."

"OK, let's do something else then."

Mr. Hess made Martin walk up and down the room several times and let him bend over forwards and backwards from his hips, which he was able to do, but only clumsily. Mr. Hess also made him say a long stretched "Aaaa", and while Martin did so, Mr. Hess gently touched the muscles on both sides of his throat, and the sound Martin created changed into a scream. But as soon as Mr. Hess released his fingers, the scream ended.

"That's fine, Mr. Fox. Let's sit down again."

Martin felt nausea creeping up from his stomach. He sat down, quivering slightly while putting his dark blue socks as well as his black cashmere pullover back on. He started to tap his right leg to soothe his nerves.

"Mr. Fox, as far as I can tell, your body is not grounded and the way you breathe doesn't provide you with enough energy. Furthermore your body signals serious inhibitions and tension, especially in the region of the throat, the waist and the pelvis. Plus your way of moving shows a strong fear of falling. The stage your body is in is far from healthy and being able to perform to the best of your natural abilities."

Martin swallowed but remained silent.

"Mr. Fox, please have a look at these five statements and tell me which ones ring true to you?" He handed Martin a sheet of paper. Martin recollected himself enough to be able to read it.

I survive better if I am all on my own.

I only allow you to come close to me as long as you look up to me.

I am free, as long as I don't lose my head and don't allow love to rule me.

If I obey you, you have to love me.

As long as I am dependent, I receive support and warmth.

"Two apply to me. I don't allow anyone to be close to me who I feel is in any aspect superior to me or even on eye level. For sure this applies to everyone at work but also to my wife, my son, and even my best friend, Hans."

"And which is the second statement that applies to you, Mr. Fox?"

"I am free as long as I don't lose my head. I hate people who are dominated by their emotions, these cuddly teddy bears who want love and compassion to lead the way."

"What bothers you about that?"

"Let's face it: life is a struggle, Mr. Hess. You don't get anywhere in life without fighting for your fair share of things. My son has this teddy bear tendency. When he was small, it was kind of cute. He carefully trapped wasps that had found the way into the house with a glass and a sheet of paper, carried them outside and let them free. Whereas I just killed these annoying creatures with a strike of the newspaper. I always told Christopher to toughen up –"

"Sound like your son had a hard time with you as a father."

"My son is a softy. Writes poems. No real man writes poems. But at least he competes in poetry slams now."

"Childhood is not meant be pre-military service, Mr. Fox."

"My father saw that differently."

"Well, that might explain a few things."

"If you have completed your diagnosis, I'd rather not keep you busy any longer," Martin said annoyed and crossed his arms.

"My diagnosis, in a few words, is quite simple. You have deteriorated from your natural healthy state into a creature that is dominated by control and performance and that likes to fight and win. If I was to use a medical term to describe your state, I'd say you behave like a rigid psychopath, and your body inhibitions and sensations confirm that from a bio-energetic point of view."

Martin's mouth fell open and he gasped. It took him some time to recollect himself. "I'm not a psychopath." He shook his head in disbelieve. "How dare you call me that?" he added, pointing his finger at Mr. Hess.

"From a medical point of view, your behaviour is that of a rigid psychopath."

"What you say is no proof to me at all."

"Your hands and feet are cold, Mr. Fox. Mine are warm. Do you have an explanation for that?"

"I've just gotten out of bed after three days with a high fever."

"The energy from the core of my body is flowing freely to the periphery, that is to say to my hands and feet as well as to my head and penis. The energy of your core is only flowing to your head where it overpowers the rest of your body. Your head controls everything else. Your body is unable to naturally release this stress created by your thinking as you are not grounded. I guess you also suffer from a serious sleeping disorder and an inability to relax and enjoy life."

"You can't compare our lives. I'm a top manager working an exhausting pace of twelve to fourteen hours a day, having to stay analytical and above things."

"My office is open six days a week, I put in some sixty hours, and I also have to be factual and analytical. But I don't pretend to be anything I'm not."

"If I would work only locally and without any air conditioning like you, I'd be as fit as you in no time."

"You're kidding yourself."

"I bet you a thousand Euros I'm not. You're roughly seven or eight years older than me. I can become as vibrant and fit as you again in just a few weeks."

Rupert Hess's face broke out in a smile.

"First, I don't need to take your money, Mr. Fox, by accepting your bet. Secondly, thanks for the compliment. Actually, I'm sixty-two. And yes, if you are willing to free yourself from all that is not naturally you but a self-chosen defence and self-marketing system, you'll be able to become as healthy and radiant as I am. But it will take you at least some two to three years."

Martin had lost his wit and his steam. He gazed into the garden, chewing on the inside of his right cheek and worrying what lay ahead of him. He slipped his hands into his trouser pockets and asked with a shaky voice, "What would I have to do for a start? I mean hypothetically? "

"I would ask you to come to see me once a week for some two hours for a couple of months. Two thirds of the time we will be working on your body, including massages of the fine muscle fibres. We need to relax them to free you from being petrified. A lot of discomfort and challenge is involved, but you are strong-willed enough to be able to master that. And I would ask you to reflect on yourself every day and keep a dairy of all of that."

"What is productive in writing notes about that?"

"It is the key to effective self-reflexion, Mr. Fox. Writing your reflexions down means you must put them into exact words. When reading them again, your awareness deepens. And when you re-read them after a longer period of time, hopefully you will be able to smile about them because you realize that you've made progress. This gives you energy to move on even more vigorously."

"Any suggestion where I could start if I decided to?"

"Write down all sentences you use that start with 'I must…' and then transform each of them into sentences that start with 'I can…' or 'I may…'. Also take notes on how specific sentences make you feel."

"OK, I'll think about that."

"I can only help you to help yourself if you're serious about this, Mr. Fox. If not, please don't waste my time."

Martin's lips parted. He looked straight at Mr. Hess while his posture relaxed more and more. He felt a sudden desire to end the distance he had created with Mr. Hess and draw on his energy.

"I'm sorry, Mr. Hess. I didn't mean to be rude. What swept over me like a giant wave a few days ago has just been totally unexpected and a bit too much."

"My part is to help Mr. Fox, not to judge. You're not the only one who finds his way to me by recommendation and who is totally sceptical at the beginning."

"I have no idea any more how it feels to be healthy, how it feels to live a joyful life. Everything has become a routine, is rather mechanical. I'm constantly on the run. I race and chase all the time," Martin said, glancing at the garden outside.

"You were not born that way."

"I can't remember."

"When you were born, Mr. Fox, your movements were nimble, supple and flowing. You were filled with love and gave love freely, to yourself, to your body and to others. You smiled, laughed and cried, danced, clapped your hands and jumped around. You expressed our needs and feelings spontaneously because your heart beat freely and without any worries. Your breath was deep, and therefore your whole body was filled with oxygen and energy. You were full of joy and vigour and in good health. Your eyes were shiny, your body felt toasty warm, your skin was bathed in a warm tone. All body fluids in bloodstreams, cells, glands and lymph nodes flew effortlessly."

"I can't remember. I can recall my son being like that when he was two or three years old. But I can't recall it from my own early childhood," Martin said with a numb feeling inside.

"I'm sure initially you were open-minded towards others and towards life as well. The energies of our bodies were once directed towards the outside and others. You were yourself and you looked well. You were able to fall asleep and into the arms of someone else free of any fears and effortlessly."

"How do you know that, Mr. Hess?"

"Because we were all born that way."

Martin smiled for the first time today. There was hope. In his mind he saw Christopher falling asleep in Helens arms after he had exhausted himself playing around with his toys or exploring the bushes and flowers in the garden. Martin had always enjoyed watching that. But he rarely was home to see it. He tried to remember how he had behaved when he was a toddler or pre-schooler. But he had no images, no memories of that, only emptiness.

"I can't remember when I allowed myself to fall asleep easily or fall into the arms of someone, I have to admit," he told Mr. Hess with a sadness that clouded his whole demeanour.

"There's a reason for that, Mr. Fox. From the time we grow in the womb until about the age of ten, our harmony gets seriously disrupted. We encounter painful life experiences. Our needs of love, tenderness, care and unity are not met the way we want or need it. In order to avoid such painful experiences in the future, we develop defence mechanisms. Controlling others and the situation is just one example."

"Something like a strategy not to get hurt again? It that what you're saying?"

"Yes, exactly, Mr. Fox. For some of us it even boils down to a feeling of needing to survive."

Survive, Martin thought while touching his throat with his right hand. Yes, that was how it had felt when his father had examined him appraisingly time and time again.

"Without noticing it, Mr. Fox, we build up our very own inner defence system and we keep living it as adults in our private and professional lives. It consists of thoughts, words and evasive behaviours. All of this is also imprinted into our body's tissue. This defence system hardens our body, in the truest sense of the word. It places a protective muscle shield around us, especially around our heart. Without being aware of it, we let the abilities of our heart be taken out of our tool box to handle life."

Martin lowered his head when scenes of his past came back to him. "I had many such experiences, Mr. Hess." He swallowed a couple of times and his hands became damp. "But I never faced up to them, especially not in front of my father. He was an officer with the British Rhine Army. To him, I always had to prove that I'm strong and assertive – that I'm worthy to call myself his son."

Images of his father forcing him to come along on 15-mile field marches when he was just ten years old, coming home with bleeding blisters on his feet and overhearing comments to his mother about him being a sissy rather than a man, rose in Martin's mind. "Just thinking about it makes me feel extremely uncomfortable, Mr. Hess." He bit his lips and needed to take a few deep breaths before Mr. Hess could continue and get his attention again.

"Do you have any idea what you did to avoid such painful experiences again?"

"No. I couldn't escape my father when he was around."

"You pushed the feelings aside and sought refuge in your thinking."

"Why should I have done that?"

"Only feelings hurt, Mr. Fox."

"But that alone doesn't help."

"That's why you also constructed a reality in your mind that made you believe you can control things. If you can control things, there won't be any more surprises that will hurt your feelings."

"Isn't it natural to want to feel safe and secure?"

"For you, the way to feeling safe was to divert from being alive and spontaneous. Your feelings were substituted by thinking."

"So what? Big deal."

"If you confine yourself to thinking you can be happy – well, then just enjoy what's happening and what you're having."

"So?"

"But if things don't happen the way you want them to happen or you don't get what you want –"

"– then I'm frustrated and fight even harder to get it," Martin completed the sentence and exhaled deeply.

"Joy, by contrast, comes from within. It never ends, it's yours all the time. Have you ever replaced the feeling of deep inner connectedness to others with the happiness of achievements or rewards, like sports medals, academic titles, cars, watches, women – ?"

Martin had to wipe his eyes when he thought of his time with Hans. He thought of the periodical evenings he and Hans had spent watching movies together. How they used to hang around in jazz clubs, drinking whiskey while joking around. His eyes became wet when he remembered how he had played hide-and-seek with Christopher when he was about three, and how much fun it had been when Christopher had jumped into his arms after he had discovered the boy hiding in a bush or behind a tree. Martin wiped his eyes again as if he wanted get a clear picture of himself that got blurred by some hazy veil. He rose. "Thank you, Mr. Hess. I need a few days to think about all this."

CHAPTER 11

Martin went for a long walk in a park close to Hans's home, trying to digest what both Hans and Mr. Hess had told him today. Round after round he walked on a pebbled food path, circling a small lake while enjoying the sunshine and the blossoming trees. The evidence was overwhelming, but how could he get out of it quickly and smartly? He was unable to find an answer that was to his liking. He didn't know how long it had taken him until his stomach started to growl. According to his watch it was 7 pm. Martin texted to Hans: 'Home in 30', will bring our favourite pizza from boarding school. Chill a few bottles of beer.'

When he walked into the kitchen, Hans was already in blue jeans and a blue-and-white striped shirt. He had set the table with plates, silverware, two bottles of cold beer and glasses.

"I warn you, Martin, your stomach isn't going to like this."

Martin dropped a carton with a giant Diavolo pizza on the table and Hans opened it. The smell of it filled the kitchen and their mouths started to water.

"At least stay away from the red chilli peppers, will you?" Hans suggested, placing a large slice on Martin's plate while Martin poured the beer into the glasses.

"Don't worry, my stomach's fine."

They sat down and ate silently for a while. Hans wrinkled his nose, tilting his head from side to side, looking at Martin to attract his attention.

"Rupert Hess is a great therapist, isn't he?" he said.

Martin just kept on eating while Hans gazed at him intensively. Finally Hans dropped his fork, reached across the table and tapped the back of Martin's right hand.

"Rupert Hess is a great therapist, isn't he?"

Martin helped himself to another slice of pizza, and Hans started fidgeting.

Irritated by his movements, Martin looked at his friend.

"If you think so –"

"Open your mouth and tell me what you think about him."

"Can't you let me finish dinner?"

"What's wrong? Usually, it's impossible to make you shut up."

"OK, OK. If you really want to know: he branded me a rigid psychopath. He said I have degenerated from a human being into a far-from-healthy rational being that blocks out its feelings. He said I'm a walking corpse, out of touch with reality, running on an autopilot of petrified survival strategies I developed as a child."

"He didn't say that."

"Well, sort of."

"And by that you mean…?"

"Get me in shape again. Next week I'll go back to work."

Hans got up and opened the dishwasher, his Adam's apple bobbing. He felt the urge to smack Martin, but his manners did not allow for that.

"We'll see." Hans said instead, disenchanted.

Martin went upstairs into his small but comfortable guestroom and dropped on his queen size bed, kicking off his shoes one by one with the other foot. He felt a sharp pain in his stomach, and acid bits that tasted like pizza dough with tomato sauce and cheese, ham, mushrooms, all spiced up with red hot pepper dipped in wheat beer pushed up his gullet. He got up as the nausea increased and barely made it to the bathroom before he threw up the acidic mixture. It took him fifteen minutes to make it back to bed, sweating, feeling hot and miserable. For a moment he thought about shouting or texting Hans for help. But then he felt too embarrassed to show Hans how miserable he felt. After about half an hour he got up again, brushed his teeth, took a shower and went into bed. His body was burning up. He drank a few sips of plain water from the bottle on the nightstand and fell into a befuddled sleep. At 10:50 pm he woke up again. His T-shirt was soaked with sweat, as were his boxer shorts. He switched on the lamp on the nightstand and climbed out of bed. Then he opened his duffel bag, pulled out a fresh T-shirt and underwear and changed into them.

On top of his clothes in the duffel bag he saw his black notebook, the one he used to take notes in important meetings. He had taken it with him to Hans in case he could start working again on some strategic ideas he had on his mind. But now an inner urge he couldn't quite place made him take it out and fetch a ball-pen from the writing desk by the window. He went back into bed, stuffed a pillow behind his back for comfort and leaned against the wall. Then he opened the notebook on the first empty page, crossed it out and turned the page. The moment he put the pen down, it seemed to start writing all by itself.

I must be successful

I must be in control

I must win

I must hide my feelings and emotions

I must achieve my goals

I must fight

I must perform

I must never give up

I must work all day long

I must be strong

I must be invincible

I must preserve

I must give my best

I must be the one others can lean on

I must do things my way

Before he knew it, he had filled the first page. He leaned back and looked at the page, reading the sentences slowly one by one as if drinking an old single-malt whiskey. Yes, that's him. He smiled, but the wrinkles around his mouth triggered a coarse and unpleasant feeling deep down inside. He felt flat out and exhausted, but something inside of him didn't feel like stopping now. His pen started to write once again.

I must be successful and changed it into *I am grateful to be successful*

I must be in control became *I might be in control*

I must win turned into *I can win*

Martin blew his nose with a paper tissue. His whole body felt funny. His brain was shouting 'no, no, no', whereas his hands, feet and cheeks were tingling with excitement. He picked up his pen again.

I must hide my feelings and emotions

He paused to drink some water

I may show my feelings and emotions

Martin looked at the two sentences as if they were aliens from a different galaxy. Would that be a safe thing to do? No. Allowing for that would mean total defeat, he decided. He dropped pen and notebook on the floor and switched off the light. Once he had settled into a more or less comfortable sleeping positions, tears started to roll down his cheeks. He wiped them away with both hands. His muscles felt weak, and his stomach was still churning. He searched for a feeling, but he couldn't detect any emotion. 'Empty,' he thought before falling into a restless sleep.

The next two days he spent in bed with fever again and getting on Hans's nerves because he kept pitying himself.

CHAPTER 12

Hans and Christopher sat at the kitchen table and had latte macchiato and fruit salad with yoghurt for breakfast when they heard Martin taking a shower upstairs.

"The diagnosis I confidentially shared with you as a future colleague over the phone Sunday morning is not quite right any more, Christopher," Hans said with a severe look on his face.

"You mean there's more to it than just high cholesterol, reflux and high blood pressure?"

"Hypertension and cholesterol levels show a high likelihood of arteriosclerosis, which will lead to cerebral thrombosis or coronary artery disease soon."

"How did he take it?"

"Like an ostrich – head in the sand. Wants me to prescribe medication so that he can do business as usual."

Christopher looked down. Then he muttered, "Sounds like Dad" and threw his hands up as if to say "I give up". He looked at Hans and asked impulsively, "Why couldn't you have been my dad?"

Hans was totally caught by surprise. His mouth fell open. "I'd rather be a cool godfather than a so-so father."

"But don't you think you would've done much better than Dad?"

"Who knows, Christopher, who knows?"

"You always made me feel alive. We watched so many movies together, sharing popcorn with salt. We sat in the garden, looking at a rainbow across the sky when the rain had just vanished and the sun came back. You wanted to read all my poems as soon as the ink had dried. You took me out to my first jazz concert. You came to visit me in medical school just after my first month there to check on me –"

Hans nodded emphatically. How he wished he had a son like Christopher.

"To your father, the rainbow has just been black and white for many years. But I can assure you he wasn't always like that. Why do you think your mother had fallen in love with him, hmmm?"

"He's always been as insensitive to my needs and feelings as NATO barbed wire is to the skin. And I guess that's true for mum's feelings as well."

Hans swallowed, deeply sad to hear his beloved godson saying this. "I know, Christopher, he confuses love with money and the meaning of life with ticking the boxes of a checklist of worldly and short-lived achievements."

"Sometimes I wonder," Christopher said, wrinkling his nose while rubbing his cheeks, "if the whole business world isn't merely a large sanatorium of occupational therapy for men like Dad."

"Would you consider switching your major to business psychiatry after graduation?" Hans joked to lighten up the situation.

Christopher smiled and exhaled through his nose. They heard sluggish steps coming down the stairs.

"Good morning, Dad. I hope you feel better," Christopher said when Martin entered the room and got up to greet his father. Martin rubbed the back of his neck.

"Christopher, I didn't hear the door bell ring."

"You couldn't have. I arrived late last night together with uncle Hans after the vernissage and the dinner party."

Martin hugged him in a clumsily distant manner. "I'm just happy to see you, son." He looked around, patted Hans on the back and added, "Just let me get my first espresso and I'll be with you both."

"Christopher wants to know if there's anything he could do to make you feel better, Martin." Hans got up to leave for his surgery.

"No, I'm just a little out of steam. A few more days of rest and I'll be back to normal."

Bullshitting as usual, Christopher thought. I'll give you a reality check now.

"Fine, Dad. I'm sure you at least want to see some pictures of last night –"

Christopher opened his blue daypack, took out his laptop and opened it.

"Don't you want to see the pictures, Hans?" Martin asked.

"I don't need to see them. I was there to enjoy them, remember?"

Martin sat down at the table besides Christopher, and his son started off with a photo of a huge oil canvas. "What do you think about this one, Dad?" Christopher asked proudly. It showed the back of a small boy with fair hair, five or six years old, who was kneeling next to a wounded coloured child of about the same age. The boy held the child's head with one hand while gently holding a glass of water to the child's lips with his other hand. You could only see the gaunt, tired face of the child in need. The terror he went through, his bruises, scars and dried-up lips, but also his big brown eyes that were full of gratitude and hope, while he was looking at the white boy who was tending to his needs. Martin got goose pimples just looking at the picture.

"She painted that for me, Dad. The little boy who is taking care of the other boy is me."

Martin looked at the boy again. Yes, he did look like Christopher when he had been little.

"I don't quite understand, son –"

"For years and years, Dad, I had the same dream. I was about that age and cared for a wounded and exhausted child. This gave me a feeling of deep satisfaction, and I knew that this was what my life is about. Later, I was able to describe the scene to Mum many times. How the child looked like in my dream, how I felt and what inspiration I draw from it for my medical studies every day. She painted it for me. But when this opportunity came to show it to the public at the art gallery, I was more than happy not to claim it for myself."

The next photo showed a sign adjacent to the painting: Mercy – Helen Meister – € 15,000 and a red dot.

"Hold it, son – does that mean this oil painting of Helen's sold for that much money?"

"Yes, Dad, isn't that wonderful? And the second one sold for the same amount, too. Here, take a look."

But Martin didn't look at the screen to see the second painting. He stared at the floor, frowning.

"Dad, look, it get's even better –" Christopher raised his voice and hit his father' upper arm to get his attention once more.

"That's George Bergan, with his arms around Helen and Anna. What is he doing there?"

"Anna is the famous painter Annaick Verstraeten, and George is Anna's husband. Mum and I have been to their wedding two years ago."

Martin nearly stopped breathing and swallowed hard. His Adam's apple danced up and down.

The next photo showed Helen linking arms with a delicately handsome man in his early fifties. He wore a perfectly tailored dark blue suit, as Martin could tell at one glance. A light green silk handkerchief with purple dots in the breast pocket and a white shirt gave him a classy look. He had a moderate suntan and immaculately coiffed hair.

"I thought Cary Grant was dead."

"He is, Dad. Alexander looks just like him."

"Who's Alexander, son?"

"Mum's new love. A business man from Hamburg. I like him a lot. He adores Mum. I'm so happy for her. They love and care about each other so much. Ask Uncle Hans! He spent nearly the whole dinner chatting with him and George."

Martin shrugged and tried to clear his throat while rubbing his lips.

"And I've made a new friend Dad."

He showed a photo of himself sitting next to Mr. Kennedy, who put his arm around him, both all smiles.

"Hmm, er" was the only thing Martin could say with narrowed eyes. He couldn't believe what he just saw and tapped his fist against his lips, exhaling through the nose.

"You know, Dad, if I could adopt a grandfather, it would be him. We talked about poetry and the poetry slam I will participate in next week. And you know what?"

"Are you talking to me?" Martin replied absent-mindedly, thinking about what George and Mr. Kennedy must think about him now.

"He invited me to come to see him in Dublin for the Curiosity Festival in a few weeks."

Martin's face darkened. He clenched his fists in anger. "Since when have you known that George is my new boss, son?" Martin felt that he was losing more and more control over his reactions.

"It's none of my business, Dad," Christopher replied calmly.

"It was your duty to tell me." Martin raised his voice.

"No." Christopher stood his ground. "It was always you telling Mum and me that we don't understand anything about your work and what's important in business."

"This is not a way to talk to your father, Christopher," Martin shouted, getting up.

Christopher stood up as well. He didn't want to look up to his father any more. "It's about time that I talk to you like this. I'm a grown man and will stand on my own two feet shortly."

"How dare you address me like that?"

"We're not in the army and I am not a trooper you order around like you do in the company. I'm your son. But you've hardly ever shown any affection for me."

"I paid for your comfortable life."

"That doesn't give you the right to keep hurting my feelings."

Martin didn't know what to say to that. He touched his throat and looked down.

"Here is a question that has troubled me at night for years. And maybe you can truthfully answer it now."

Martin stared at Christopher. He was unable to comprehend that his son really made a demand on him.

"Would you have married Mum if she hadn't been pregnant with me?"

Martin's palms began to sweat. He took a deep breath and felt checkmated. What should he say? Be honest and hurt him once more – or tell a lie and run the risk that Christopher would realize the truth anyway and turn away from him for the rest of his life? After a few moments of pondering, Martin said, "I felt obliged to."

Christopher flushed and dry washed his hands, cramping them together. "So your life with Mum was a lie?"

Sweat ran down Martin's neck. He didn't know what to reply.

"Thank you, Dad." Christopher closed his laptop and put it in his backpack. "I'll need time to digest this. Please understand. I'll be in touch when I feel like I can talk to you. Good-bye, Dad." He shot his father a long pained look and turned to leave without as much as a hand-shake. Christopher was unable to find any sympathy for his father right now. He opened the door and walked out with drooping shoulders.

Minutes passed by in which it dawned on Martin what had hit him. Then his aggressive impatience took over once again. He grabbed his mobile phone and pushed the short dial number 5. "Helen …," he said reproachfully and harshly, "since when has George Bergan known that I'm your husband, and what else does he know?"

"Good morning, Martin. Let me think. He has known that I'm married to a Dr. Martin Fox since he started dating Anna some three years ago. He learned that you didn't want to attend their wedding two years ago. He knows that I've had the intention to leave you for about a year. Actually, it was Anna who helped his best friend, Alexander, and me to come together. He eventually met you when he took over as CEO. Yes, that's as brief as I can put it."

"Hellleeeennnn," Martin shouted into the phone as hard as he could. "I – hate – you."

Helen pulled the phone away from her ear in an attempt to protect her eardrum. When he fell silent again, she said softly, "Is it my fault that you misjudged who I am connected to? Is it my fault that you suffer from social-emotional autism? I don't think so. I've never spoken badly about you. Regaining my self-confidence required learning other things – not making you look bad or small. Bye, Martin." Shaking her head, she rang off.

Martin broke out in a hot sweat. He needed to talk to Hans. Now. What had Hans known since last night? He knocked on the door of the surgery and opened it. Fortunately, there was no patient with his friend at that moment.

"Hans, you met George Bergan, Mr. Kennedy and Helen's lover, Alexander, last night, didn't you?" he asked in a voice that sounded like a drill sergeant on a bad day.

"Yes, I did, Martin. Great guys. It was a real pleasure chatting with them."

"Did you talk about me?"

"Not a single word."

Acid burned in Martin's throat. He clenched his fists. It seemed as if he didn't matter at all any more.

"What did you talk to George about?"

"Well, if you really want to know – I asked him about the story of the tax-evading CFO that went through the press and how he would solve it."

"And what did he say?"

"He told me that the only potentially suitable person from inside the company had not dared to throw his hat into the ring so far and that they're looking outside now."

Martin walked up und down Hans' surgery, unable to calm down, while Hans sat in his chair like a rock.

"Martin. Come here and sit down for a moment," he ordered in a firm voice and pointed to the patient's chair right in front of him. Martin obeyed reluctantly.

"Your behaviour is disgusting, my friend."

Ashamed, Martin looked down. He knew Hans was right.

"Part of your conversation with Christopher in the kitchen got so loud that even I could overhear it from here. You also shouted at Helen, over the phone, I guess."

"Yes." Martin hung his head.

"Not everybody else's life revolves exclusively about your needs and wants. When will that finally begin to sink in?" Hans said, raising his voice.

Martin remained silent, holding his head with both hands as if he needed to support himself from falling over.

"I expect you to apologize to both, Helen and Christopher, immediately." Martin knew that his friend was right but he didn't want to admit it.

"But they should have told me about George, shouldn't they?"

"First you call them idiots, and then you want them to manage your career? Maybe Rupert Hess should check on whether you also suffer from schizophrenia."

Martin frowned. Though his eyes were wide open, they became perfectly motionless. Then he got up and left the room with jerky steps to go upstairs.

"And if there are others you owe an apology, it would be a good opportunity to make a clean sweep now," Hans added with a firm undertone.

He could hear Martin's footsteps on the staircase to the first floor. A door opened and shut, and then there was silence.

Martin fell on his bed and started to cry. For several minutes, he couldn't stop sobbing. He grabbed his hair and pulled it, trembling all over, shouting into the pillow, "'No, no, no –"

After about fifteen minutes he started to calm down. He grabbed his smart-phone and texted to Christopher: *I love you, Son, and I don't want to lose you!* He stared at the display, waiting for a reply. Nothing. He had just done what a man on a mission to make it to the top would do, hadn't he? So what was wrong with that? Why couldn't they see that he needed some appreciation for what he did, too?

Bling bling. Martin blinked and looked at the display. Christopher replied: *It's about time you learn to apologise!* Martin's mouth fell open. He pressed his left hand against his throat, feeling dizzy for a moment. Then he collected himself and texted: *I am sorry, Son. I never meant to hurt your feelings and I never meant to hurt your mum.*

Bling bling it sounded again. *Give me time to digest everything, Dad. I'll be in touch soon.*

A slow smile appeared on Martin's face. He dropped his smartphone, looked up and pressed his palms to his heart. "I need to fix this," he said to himself. "I really need to fix this." His mouth felt dry. He picked up the water bottle and took a long sip. He pondered who else he owed an apology … Yes, the young managers of the Strategic Task Force Next Generation Leaders. He picked up his smartphone again and wrote an e-mail to Thomas, Emma, and Zhang Ai.

Hello,

I would like to apologise for my behaviour during our meeting last Thursday. I didn't mean to be disrespectful or attack you personally. I appreciate your work, the clarity of your thoughts and standpoints as much as your courage to stand up for it. I am just as eager to see George succeed.

Best, Martin

For a moment his finger hesitated, but then it pushed the 'Send' button. A deep sense of relief spread through his whole body. He swallowed hard.

CHAPTER 13

Martin rejoiced when he pushed the revolving door and stepped into the entrance hall of headquarters. After slightly over two weeks he was back in familiar territory, but something felt different right away. The main wall of the entrance hall had been redecorated, and the work still seemed to continue. The huge flashy marketing campaign photos of their products and applications, featuring happy-looking children and adults, had gone. They had been replaced by a large oil canvas with one woman and children on the left side of the wall. On the right side a text of about the same size was painted on the wall. Both were surrounded by a field dipped in night-light with some kind of fiery red explosion in the distance. The field extended the oil canvas so it covered the whole wall. Curiously, he stepped across the entrance hall to get a closer look. The canvas showed an Indian woman in her early thirties; she was kneeling and holding one baby in her arm, pressed to her breast, while two small children crouched together next to her on an open field at nightfall. Their eyes screamed with fear, horror and helplessness. Their faces were dirty and their clothes were torn and stained with blood. Looking at it, Martin got goose pimples. A small sign to the right-hand side of the painting read: 'Bhopal – Helen Meister – 2015'.

Martin started to shiver from head to toe. He swallowed and

broke out in a sweat. After a while he moved over to the text and read:

TODAY

A child of God,

I stand here, silent.

A child of God,

I cry.

The Earth is torn

By my own making –

I partook in every way

by what I did

or

did not do

as abuse won out the day.

A child of God,

I lift my prayers,

My sleeves rolled up in service.

Abuse stops here.

A new world is built.

It starts

with me

today.

On a tiny plate at the right-hand side of the poem it read:

'Today' – Sharon K. Richards – Word Songs from my soul II – 2015.

Martin exhaled deeply. He turned away and made his way upstairs with the lift. Visibly shaken and bleak, he arrived in Karin's office. She stared at him.

"You look like a train has just run you over."

"That's exactly how I feel. I had a closer look at the new decoration in our entrance hall. Bring me a glass of water and leave me a few minutes on my own, please."

He entered his office, laid down the briefcase, took off his jacket and loosened the tie before he dropped into his chair.

"Here you are, Dr. Fox."

Martin drank the water in one go.

"Painting and poem have already created quite a stir, I can tell you. Some managers and the Chairman of the Works Council protested against it, saying it was 'inappropriate and damaging to our company to present itself like that' and that 'the CEO's personal opinion shouldn't be our public face' – "

"That's not what's troubling me, Karin."

Karin was puzzled. "Do you still feel a little bit ill?"

She got no reply. He stared out of the window. As soon as Karin had closed the door behind her, he called his wife.

"Helen, good morning. I came to see you to apologize for all I did to you a few days ago. Why didn't you tell me that George bought one of your paintings and that I'll finally get to see it in our entrance hall?"

"Good morning, Martin. You came to me to talk about you.

You didn't even ask how I was feeling nor did you want to look at my current work or wanted to know who bought my art. As my painting is exhibited under my maiden name, you are not connected to it in public. So I don't see how you can possibly have an issue with that. You are neither related to any embarrassment nor to the success that might come with it now."

Martin swallowed. "I'm sorry, Helen. I guess it was just my usual reflex. Can you forgive me?"

Before Helen could reply, there was a knock on the door, and in his usual mode of availability he said, "Come in." Without considering Helen might still want to say something, he pushed the hang-up button on his smart phone and rose from his desk chair.

Thomas Winter, pale, with drooping shoulders, walked towards Martin with an envelope in his hand.

"I did it," he said with a shaky voice.

"Did what?"

"Falsify a lab report as proof that George is HIV positive. It's the 'evidence' that is referred to by the media."

He took the lab report out of the envelope and handed it to Martin, who looked at the document. It looked genuine.

"How the hell did you do that?"

"Easy for a computer nerd."

"But why?" Martin asked, still shaking his head.

"Family pressure." Thomas looked down and continued in a shaky voice, "My uncle said I owed him something in return. I didn't expect he would force me to become a criminal and act against my own convictions."

"But why do you owe him anything?"

"I'm his younger sister's only child. I never had a father, just a procreator. Mum brought me up all on her own, working night shifts at a dry-cleaner's to keep us alive. She died of breast cancer a few days before I turned eighteen. From that day on I've made my own living, but my uncle supported me. Whenever I couldn't make ends meet with jobs in bars while going to university, he gave me some money."

"Who else took care of you?"

"Nobody."

"So that's how you became a computer nerd?"

"I guess so. If you're lonely, the internet becomes your community."

"What kind of community?"

"Since I was ten, I found comfort in the Harry Potter books, later in the films and for several years now I've been an editor of the Harry Potter Wiki."

"How can that provide comfort?"

"Harry was an even lonelier child than me. From him I learned to be brave and courageous," Christopher said with tears in his eyes.

"From a book?"

"If you don't have a father who understands you and who can serve as your role model –"

Martin exhaled through his nostrils.

"When the first Harry Potter movie was released, I sat in the cinema all by myself. It was a few weeks shy of Christmas. My classmates had their fathers at their side, sharing popcorn, joy and excitement. There was nothing I could do about that. But I could talk to everybody about Harry's journey and how love will win in the end."

Martin exhaled deeply through his nose.

"Are you OK, Dr. Fox?"

Martin remembered that Helen had sent him to the cinema with Christopher to watch the first Harry Potter movie. But instead of enjoying it with his son, he had just bought him a bag of popcorn and a paper cup of orange juice, deposited him in a seat and gone outside to make several phone calls. When they had come home, Christopher had been in tears. Martin had thought that it had been because of the film, but later Helen had told him that his son had cried because he had felt abandoned. Martin swallowed once more and looked into Thomas's eyes.

"But why are you coming to me with this?"

"You're the first grown-up who has ever apologised to me."

Martin's eyes became soft, filled with an inner glow.

"I don't dare go to the police all on my own and turn myself in. Could you come with me, for the sake of your company and for me, please?"

Martin felt deeply touched and wiped his eyes. He put his right hand on Thomas's shoulder and thought for a moment.

"Would you come with me? Please?" Thomas repeated.

"We're not going to the police, Son. Just leave the document with me, go back to your work and stay quiet until you hear from me."

As soon as Thomas had left, utterly surprised and puzzled, Martin took the lab report and walked straight to George's office.

"I need to talk to George; it can't wait for even one minute," Martin said to George's assistant. He didn't want to have any time to think his plan over and turn away from it like a coward. He found George sitting at his desk, reading a report. George looked up in surprise as his assistant announced Martin with the words,

"It's Dr. Fox. It seems to be a matter of life and death." George stood up, walked towards Martin and shook his hand. He offered him a seat at his oval cherry-wood meeting table. Martin declined. He put the lab report on George's desk while standing across from him. George read it with widening eyes, raising his eyebrows. For a moment George was speechless.

"I did it, together with Franz Winter. I falsified this document, and he forwarded it to the local radio station that triggered all other media reports about you." Martin's body was covered in cold sweat. He saw George clenching his left hand into a fist, his whole face and demeanour tightening up. With flaring nostrils he asked, "Why do you hate me that much?"

"I take full responsibility for it. I apologize and I ask you to forgive me. I didn't mean to hurt you personally."

"What do you think you did?"

"We wanted to stop the reforms you and Mr. Kennedy have in mind. Mr. Winter fears for his powers as the Chairman of the Works Council and his seat on the Board of Directors. So far we Germans have ruled everything. Now there's Mr. Kennedy who is foreign, you are mostly foreign, the hierarchy –"

"And you aren't foreign even though you have a British father, are you?"

"The threat you pose to people like me is that you will take away everything I have struggled and strived for in my career." Martin lowered his head, awaiting his punishment while more cold sweat ran down his spine.

George walked back to his desk and dropped the lab report on his desktop. Then he leaned on the table with both hands, as if he needed to regain his balance. After a few moments that seemed like ages, in which Martin accused himself of ruining his whole career with this stupid idea of protecting Thomas, George turned around and said in a firm voice, "I forgive you and I accept your apology."

"Could you say that again?"

"I forgive you and I accept your apology."

Martin pressed his hand on his stomach and uttered softly, "Thank you. I'm deeply in your debt."

"You are, and also in that of all those who suffered from it: my wife, my family, people here in the company –"

"What can I do – besides saying I'm sorry?"

"I expect you to do your utmost to repair the damage you and Mr. Winter have caused this company."

"You're not turning me in to the police, George?"

"We all make stupid mistakes, Martin. I had my fair share of very stupid mistakes. I behaved selfishly to protect my career moves. I used to be an authoritarian manager, believing I knew it all and keeping others small to make me look even better. But worst of all, I didn't stand for anything except my own wishes and great ideas: So I fell for anything that suited me and my ideas on a short-term basis and gave a shit about what it meant to others. I lost my job, I was kicked out, and you know what? It served me right! I slowly learned what it means to take full responsibility for my deeds or omissions. And I learned how to make up for the damage I had created, be it out of out conviction or ignorance."

Martin exhaled deeply. While he briefly closed his eyes, he felt a sudden lightness in his whole body.

"Find a way to make Mr. Winter admit to it as well."

Martin looked straight into his eyes. "You can count on me, George."

He offered George his hand, and George shook it, confident that he had made the right decision.

"Thank you, George, I'll never forget that."

"I count on you. If we want to turn this company around, I need guys like you."

Back in his office, Martin called Thomas.

"I covered up for you with George and took the blame."

"What?" Thomas pressed the palm of his left hand against his cheek in sheer disbelieve. He isn't a Muggle, Thomas thought.

"Let's say I have something to make up myself."

"Thank you so much! I don't know what else to say, honestly." Tears ran down his cheeks, and he was glad that nobody could see them.

"Let's not talk about it any more, Thomas."

Thomas couldn't believe it. He exhaled, deeply relieved. "And now?"

"George pardoned me. No police. But I need your help to make up for the damage. First thing, I guess, is to stop the continuing false reporting."

That evening, Martin left the office and jumped around in the parking lot as if he was air-fencing an imaginative opponent and winning. What a day! He couldn't remember when he had last felt that great. On his way home to Hans he was humming and whistling the song Don't Worry, Be Happy in his car. He couldn't wait to tell Hans what had happened.

"That's the Martin I know from our younger days," Hans commented with a smile on his face. "I'll treat you to a pizza and a glass of red wine in my favourite restaurant around the corner."

"Thank you. But you could also share with me what George and Mr. Kennedy told you about the search for a new CFO."

"You don't give up, do you?"

"Never!"

CHAPTER 14

Martin was in high spirits. He felt physically stronger again, and his confidence was picking up a little more each day. Hans had told him repeatedly that taking pills and continuing as he used to live was not a serious option. But more out of a lack of another option than by conviction, Martin decided to pay another visit to Rupert Hess and see what kind of effect his treatment might in fact have on him.

"Here's my homework, Mr. Hess." Martin handed his notebook with the list of 'I must…' sentences over to him after they had sat down in the two comfortable chairs in the therapy room that overlooked the garden.

Mr. Hess read them carefully one by one.

"Quite a list. Wow. You had to perform for love and appreciation in your childhood like a gladiator in Rome, it seems."

"My mother loved me the way I was. She always understood me. But to my father, I was a failure. I tried so very hard to make him love me."

"What's the hardest part for you today?"

"Not being on top of things, not being good enough, admitting that I have failed and having to say 'I'm sorry'. All of this makes me sweat, shiver and swallow hard."

"In top management, your working environment is as intolerant to non-performing and loosing control as your father was. Would that be a fair statement?"

Martin shrugged. "Could you say that again?"

"Could the ruthless rules of the executive world merely have replaced the tough rules your father set for you?"

"You mean I perpetuated my childhood drama by choosing that working environment? I thought I chose this career because it suits me."

"Hmm … motherly love, Mr. Fox, is by its very nature unconditional. Mothers give us security in life with every understanding look, every loving touch, every caring support. A mother loves us because we are her children, and nothing we do can destroy that. Period. Fatherly love, by contrast, is conditional. Our father wants to teach us things about life, and we need to fulfil his expectations, follow his rules and views. If a father thinks we didn't do well, he will withdraw his love, show us we don't deserve it. Fathers with little to no empathy will usually overdo it and hurt us dreadfully."

Martin pondered, looking down at the wooden floor and then up at the ceiling. He placed the palms of his hands together, fingers pointing to heaven, and put them to his lips. "Wouldn't it be possible to rewind my behaviour to the natural state it was in before I went into the tight-jacket of my father's expectations? If that's possible, I guess I would be eager to start."

"Yes, we can turn you back into the natural Martin. But when it comes to the question of how long it will take, I have to caution you, Mr. Fox. We can trigger things to happen. We cannot force them to happen, and we can't add a timetable to them. Let go of your eagerness. Give yourself over to your body's wisdom."

"Patience and letting go of control are not my things, Mr. Hess," Martin said, shaking his head.

"Not yet, Mr. Fox, not yet. Please take off your socks and pullover, as you did last time. Don't worry, you won't be cold, you'll get warm and comfortable pretty soon. Today, I will use a vibration meditation to ground you through your legs again. That's necessary to overcome your fear of falling and, with it, of failing. Just follow my instructions and give yourself over to the movements for this hour. That's all."

Martin looked at him without knowing what to expect, but did as he was told. What did he have to lose? Nothing, he thought.

A xylophone and drum music started in a rhythmic beat that became faster and faster. Martin was asked to loosen and shake his whole body, allowing the shaking to come from the inside more and more and then let go of any control and become the shaking. Martin did as Rupert Hess had asked him to do but he felt ridiculous. He could hear his body creaking all over while he began to groan. After fifteen minutes, the sound of a flute with guitars and drums took over and Mr. Hess asked Martin to dance freely and energetically. What? Martin thought, I'm not a dancer. It felt horribly awkward. As Mr. Hess joined him, Martin became more relaxed and daring, moving across the wooden floor like a fencing dancer. Then a gong sounded, and he heard larger and smaller gongs creating a monastery-like atmosphere. Mr. Hess said, "Freeze, close your eyes, remain still, keep your back straight." Martin froze, standing only on one leg and a half. Sweat ran down his spine. The music started again, like a choral accompanied by a church organ, sweet and majestic. Thoughts rushed through his head. George, Helen, Christopher, Hans … The music changed again, now to something that sounded like an orchestra of Indian string instruments having a jam session before fading away.

"Be silent now, keep your eyes closed and sit or lie down," Mr. Hess instructed.

And silent it was, endlessly, it seemed to Martin. He had to discipline his mind every couple of seconds to make it stop from thinking without falling asleep. Martin was surprised to find how difficult that was.

"That's it for today, Mr. Fox. Well done for a first-timer. How do you feel?"

"Warm and comfortable … and loose, free and easy in a way I haven't felt for years!"

"Great."

"But how come?"

"This meditation exercise shook up your rock-like foundations so they became fluid again and brought you back in a state of natural being. It's a gentle and effective way of releasing stress and tension, reconnecting you to the earth. But it won't last very long unless you practice regularly."

Rupert Hess offered him a cup of herbal tea. "Take your time. Stay a little longer in the silence from within and then go outside and walk a few rounds in the garden to vitalize your senses as well."

The tea refreshed Martin. In the garden, he enjoyed the warm sunrays dancing on his face and the freshness of a slight breeze. He deeply breathed in and out while he was walking along the meandering pebbled path between rocks of various shapes, boxwood, camellias in full blossom as well as purple magnolia trees, black bamboo and red maple. All plants seemed so bright, just reborn, and fresh in colour and texture. He also discovered a pond full of rose-coloured water lilies and lotus as well as a stone lantern. Boston Ivy had grown miraculously alongside the open rounded windows of the pavilion. What an energizing waste of time, he thought. He took a rest on a wooden bench in the small open pond side pavilion that overlooked the most scenic spot of the water. Nothing to accomplish, just letting life in. He felt marvellous.

On his way back into the house he met a petite woman in a red shirt and blue jeans with bare feet and shiny scarlet nails, long black hair and sparkling bear-brown eyes who slowly walked towards him. She seemed relaxed and concentrated at the same tine. Was she –? Yes, Selma Adams, not doubt.

"How wonderful to see you again," she said in a soft yet firm voice and shook his hand gently.

"Yes, in – de – ed," Martin stuttered. He flushed and shook his head. He couldn't believe he acted like that.

"Are you in treatment with Mr. Hess?" Martin inquired gently, biting his lip.

"I was, for some years actually."

Martin smiled, still feeling a bit lost and insecure about this encounter. "Uh … may I ask what you've been treated for?"

"Sure. I showed the behaviour patterns of a rigid psychopath."

Martin laughed. "Mr. Hess said something similar to me."

"Join the club," she replied, chuckling.

"What made you sign up for a treatment here?"

"I smashed my laptop on the desk of my boss and then dropped it into his aquarium."

Martin's eyes widened while he took a step back.

"Don't worry, none of the fish got hurt," she added with a smile.

"Only you, I guess."

"It was my wake-up call and I needed it."

"Are you in treatment with Rupert?" she returned the question.

"Just started."

"You're in very good hands. Give yourself over. I know how difficult this is. Just dare do it." She laughed again.

"Mr. Fox, your massage," the young therapist from the treatment room called.

"Sorry, I have to go." Moving closer again, Martin took her hand and indicated a kiss.

"Will I see you here again?"

"That may very well be. I love this garden, and my daughters love it, too."

"Sorry, I have to go now." Martin passed by her on his way to the house, turning around twice to look at her again.

The massage was anything but what Martin had expected. For an hour the young man hardly touched his muscles. At one point Martin even fell asleep. What a waste of time, he thought.

"How was your afternoon, Mr. Fox?" Rupert Hess inquired when Martin was about to leave the therapist's practice.

"I have to admit, I feel a lot better, more lively – yes, that's the right word. And your garden ... just great. But the massage wasn't a massage."

"It was, but not of the kind you know. It relaxes the hardened small muscles deep inside around your heart. You'll see soon."

"Anyway, I feel great and I'm looking forward to coming back," Martin said with a flutter in his belly.

"Good, until next time, please ponder about my definition of FAIL."

Martin listened up. He moved closer. "Which is?"

"First Attempt in Learning."

"Ha ha, that's a good one." Martin slapped his thigh.

"Maybe the only sensible way to look at it? Think about it, Mr. Fox."

"May I ask you one more thing?"

"Sure."

"I met Selma Adams, the petite woman with hair as black as the night and shiny bear-eyes, in the garden."

"My warrior." He smiled.

"A warrior? No, she's the new Chief People & Ethics Officer of our company –"

"An archetype warrior." Mr. Hess laughed.

"But how can such a small woman be a warrior? She does not look physically strong. All I sense is –"

"What?"

"Might."

"There you go. And what does that tell you instinctively?"

Martin pressed his lips together. "Don't mess with her."

"Voilà."

"But do you think it's safe to get closer to her?"

Rupert Hess laughed out loud. "There's only one way to find out, Mr. Fox, only one way."

CHAPTER 15

"Karin, good morning. Get me an appointment with George as fast as you can, will you?" Martin said when he entered her office. "Today, if possible."

She was busy watering her orchids on the windowsill and made a face while shaking her head.

"You're aware of the fact that it's Friday, 10 am, right?"

"Come, on Karin, use your magic."

"You mean my credit with some people."

"Come on … I know you're friends with his assistant. Help me to get both of us into the ExCom."

"Why should I want to work even harder than now?"

Martin closed the door and went to his desk. He started to go through the pile of documents on the right-hand side of his desk. The pile had doubled during his sick leave. Oh, the investment into a new production line for specialty chemicals in Chennai... He picked up the file and started to read. Half an hour later Karin walked in.

"I got you your appointment."

"You're absolutely magnificent."

"George said if you don't mind the moving boxes, he'd be happy to welcome you at his home at 11:30 am and could spare half an hour max."

Martin beamed in anticipation. He put his hands together to stretch them with the whole arms, palms outward, cracking his knuckles.

"You owe me one," Karin said, handing him a handwritten note with George's private address.

Martin leaned back in his chair and folded his hands behind the back of his head in anticipation of success.

"By the way, did you see George's wife making a comment on his alleged HIV infection during the television interview she gave last night on the occasion of her exhibition?" Karin asked, putting her hand over her heart and licking her lips.

"What'd she say?" Martin sat up.

"She said that having sex with him was and is healthy and pleasant."

Amused, Martin smiled. "She has a good sense of humour, hasn't she, Karin?"

"If I get hold of the bastard who launched this smear campaign against George, I'll kick him in the balls."

Martin grimaced. Without saying another word, he left the office.

He had followed the instructions of his GPS and arrived in a modest neighbourhood. I must have the wrong street address, he thought.

"Damn," he shouted and hit the steering wheel with the sweaty palm of his right hand. He stopped the car in front of No. 3, a somewhat larger three-story house with a white paint coat. It had a black roof, a plain lawn and a few rose bushes in front. A small electric car sat in the driveway. He parked his car on the street, got out and looked at the doorbell. 'Bergan / Verstraeten' it read. No mistake. He exhaled. His tense shoulders relaxed.

"Let's state my claim," Martin mumbled while stretching his back and ringing the doorbell.

George opened the white wooden door with a smile. "Come on in, Martin."

He led him through the hall. They passed quite a few moving boxes that were stacked against the wall and entered a spacious living room with high windows that opened onto a small terrace with a rose garden at the back of the house. One wall of the living room was completely covered with a bookshelf filled with stacks of eight to ten large art books, which created an atmosphere of composed colour and made it easier to read the titles without twisting your neck. The other two walls were painted in eggshell and served as a background for two huge oil canvases. One painting was an abstract landscape – water and mountains in the back – in different shades of red. The other one was a portrait of an elderly woman who resembled Marlene Dietrich in her late years. Martin was stunned. He hadn't expected that. Everything, except for the paintings but including the pale wooden floor, looked plain and modest for a home of a power couple.

George had been sitting with Mr. Kennedy in the living room. Martin shook hands with the Chairman.

"I met your son, and I'm very fond of him."

"Thank you, Mr. Kennedy. I'm very proud of him."

"Would you please excuse us for half an hour?" George said and was about to guide Martin to his adjacent study.

"I don't mind if the Chairman listens – in fact, it might be a good idea," Martin intervened.

"Well, OK, then have a seat, Martin."

Martin sat down in one of the four terracotta-coloured easy-chairs across from George; Mr. Kennedy was to his right. Mr. Kennedy looked excited to be included. He fetched a small box with lemon sherbet sweets from his jacket pocket and offered them to the other two with a smile of his face. George gladly accepted one but Martin was far too nervous for that.

"No thanks, Mr. Kennedy, maybe later," he said politely.

"So what can I do for you, Martin? Have you convinced Franz Winter to admit to his campaign against me as well?"

"No, it isn't about that."

"OK, so what is it?"

"George, when I listened to your speech last week at the auditorium, I got the impression that something unheard of and beyond the imagination of most will take place in our company, starting now. We will become the beacon of a new area. And I want to be part of that in a driver's seat. I really mean it. I have commenced treatment with a well-known and highly capable body-mind-soul therapist. And I'm committed to go through this, come hell or high water. But my question to you – actually to you both – is: What do I have to do to become part of the new Executive Committee you're putting together around yourself and Selma Adams right now?"

Martin exhaled through his nostrils and leaned back. There – he had said what he had needed to say.

George and Mr. Kennedy smiled at each other and then at him. George took another glass from the side table, filled it with water from a simple glass carafe and offered it to Martin, who gladly took it. His mouth and throat felt dry.

"We're all seeking the same thing, Martin. And by that I don't mean the glory of a C-position in a major company like ours."

But what else does he believe I came for? Martin rubbed his chin.

"Deep down inside, we want to achieve the truest and highest expression of who we are."

Martin nodded although he didn't quite understand what George was saying, but he didn't want to admit that.

"We don't walk on Earth by the will of our ego, Martin. We walk on Earth by the grace of God. And this we have forgotten. And because we have forgotten it, we behave as if we ruled the world by our will and power and as if only our needs matter. That's what needs to be fixed – and fast, in our Executive Committee, too."

"OK, but how do you suggest I tackle that? Go to church more often? I'm an atheist."

"I don't care if you follow any religious faith or if you're an atheist, and neither does Mr. Kennedy. If you're an atheist, you probably live by Kant's imperative."

"Spot on."

"But if I observe your selfish and ignorant ways, I can only deduce from them that you haven't yet understood Kant properly."

Pooohhh. Martin wasn't prepared for such openness.

"You mean I haven't understood the Golden Rule? Come one, it's easy. I should treat others as I want them to treat me."

"Not entirely. It's not an empty algorithm in which you can fill in all kinds of egocentric wants. If I accept to be beaten, I can – according to that rule – beat others without hurting my own morals. That's why Jesus and Kant filled the Golden Rule with a specific meaning and purpose in order to protect it from abuse."

Martin looked away. He hid his hands in his pocket and visibly blushed.

"Martin, what love is to religion, human dignity is to Kant. Christianity, for example, fills the so-called Golden Rule with loving our neighbours the way we love ourselves. Kant wants us to treat all human being with the same dignity. He fills the gap of the Rule with his famous vision of humanity as a whole. In each single person, humanity as a whole is at stake. Both start from the assumption that all is one and that we're all one."

Martin knew he couldn't pretend that he was living that. Probably he didn't even love himself. And human dignity, well, he didn't care about that either. Flustered, he lowered his gaze.

"I need leaders, Martin, who are willing and able to fulfil their highest potentials. I need refined and fully self-aware characters in action, who have little concern about themselves and a lot of concern about everyone else."

"I guess it'll be tough for head-hunters for top management positions to find that category."

"That's our problem. A bag full of skills, a bucket full of experience and a checklist full of achievements won't do. Self-aware and mature people like Selma Adams are hard to find, much harder than money and investors."

"But where and how do you find them?"

"I found George by asking around with people in the industry, 'Who failed miserably?'" Mr. Kennedy replied.

"But that's stupid. Who wants a failure? And who will admit to having failed?"

"Healthy leaders of the kind we're looking for, Martin. They mess up, realize it and refine themselves out of their own strong desire because deep down inside they've understood something."

"Well, I guess I don't fit into that category," Martin said, half-joking in an attempt to get over the awkward situation.

"Not yet, Martin, not yet. You're still full of fears – not love or human dignity – in one way or another. That's why you scored high in the five clusters of sick behaviours in the first place."

Martin hadn't expected to hear that, and he was still trying to make sense of what George had said. Coming here, he had hoped for a clear-cut 'Yes, you're in if you can prove to me that you can manage this particular problem we have with xyz'. And now this! He hung his head in defeat.

"Martin," Mr. Kennedy added, "you need to learn how to remain rooted in love and care in places that scare you and where you usually would fight others, turning a blind eye on the damage you create. You need to stay calm and composed in situations in which you loose control, and pay attention to where this loss of control takes you. Once you're able to do that, you will be ready for our ExCom."

George looked at him with a gentle and affectionate smile. "Rest assured," he added, moving forward in his chair, "I'll do all I can to support you on this path, Martin. But it's up to you to be courageous and refine yourself first."

Martin gasped for breath. This hurt. He drank more water.

"Is there any chance I will become the next CFO?" he asked. He wanted to show them how firm he was in his resolve to make it to the ExCom.

"Nope," Mr. Kennedy replied and leaned towards him with a fatherly smile. "It'll take time for you to become yourself again."

"But couldn't I do both simultaneously? I mean Peter Stark's team runs the whole thing, it's a well-oiled machine."

"The way we handle our finances needs to be straightened out as well. It goes against our values and is unethical. We need to stop living at the cost of others now. Just think of our payment terms for our smaller suppliers."

"Peter Stark wasn't a refined character either, Mr. Kennedy."

"True, but his fall gives me a chance to place a person in this crucial position now who has already progressed on his way to a healthy leader."

"Do you really think its possible to implement an ethical Three Generations Perspective in our business, become profitable again and change the rules of the industry by walking that path?"

"Did you watch the Star Wars movies?" Mr. Kennedy wanted to know.

"All of them. I love them."

"Do you remember the scene when Luke Skywalker had sunk his jet in the swamp of Dagobah, and Master Yoda asked him to pull it out with the power of his mind connecting to the Force?"

"Yes, Mr. Kennedy, Luke failed. He said, 'I can't. It's too big.

You want the impossible'."

"Yes. And when Yoda had pulled it out with his mind, what did Luke say?"

"I can't believe it."

"And what did Yoda reply?"

"That is why you fail."

That brought a smile to Martin's face. This jolly old man had just taught him a lesson he could have learned on his own some time ago.

"What I need in the ExCom, Martin, are modern Yodas. You're a Luke, not ready yet. There's still too much of the Dark Side active inside you."

"What do I have to do?" Martin picked up his game.

"Let your old rules die, you must." Mr. Kennedy said and laughed out loud, proud of how well he had imitated Yoda's somewhat strange speech pattern.

"I got it, Mr. Kennedy."

The three looked at each other in silence for a moment.

"We need you desperately, Martin. Get ready and find yourself," George said.

"Thank you. I appreciate your honesty and encouragement."

"Next Tuesday at 10 am I have a meeting with the Strategic Work Force Next Generation Leaders. You're welcome to join me."

"I'll be happy to take this opportunity."

George walked Martin back to the front door. When they were about to shake hands, he said, "Now I have a confession to make."

Martin lifted his eyebrows.

"Since last night I've known that you haven't falsified the lap report."

"What do you mean? Of course I did."

"No, Thomas Winter did. And that also explains why you haven't made any progress in convincing Franz Winter to admit to his campaign against me. You were never part of the plot."

"How do you know?"

"Thomas came to see me and told me the whole story. He apologized and asked for forgiveness. Martin, I really admire how you meant to protect that young gifted man and put yourself at risk."

"Well … thank you," Martin muttered, flushing a little while his whole body started to tingle. "It's not only Thomas I did it for. I have to make up for quite a few things with the younger generation, I guess."

CHAPTER 16

George and Martin shock hands in front of the meeting room across from the CEO's office. It was 10 am sharp. George opened the door. Thomas Winter, Emma Cunningham and Zhang Ai were already sitting in a row at the rectangular wooden table for six, computer and beamer ready. They got up and shook hands. Martin sat down across from Thomas, smiling at him as they were partners in crime. He caught himself thinking why he hadn't been blessed with such a rationally thinking son as Thomas.

"OK. guys. I'm curious about how you think we should do business in the future and how we should evaluate what we do. Who will start?"

"I will," Zhang Ai said, starting the computer and getting the beamer going. She was a tall woman for Chinese standards, had a friendly round face with broad cheekbones, brown eyes and a sensual mouth, framed by long black hair parted in the middle of her large skull. Zhang Ai was dressed in black; her outfit was only accentuated by a dark grey scarf with a red-and-crème cross-pattern round her neck. All of this gave her a darkish, serious look.

"Our mission should simply be to Serve People and Planet with Chemicals. We think that the following six actions are needed to set us on the right path."

She pushed the button for the first slide:

<u>Serving People and Planet with Chemicals</u>

Focus on our vision and mission;

Meet legitimate needs of people and planet;

Hold everyone accountable for living values;

Seek leaders who exercise authority;

Organise and reward collaboration;

Work in clusters and projects.

Martin and George studied the slide thoroughly.

"I expected suggestions worked out in detail, not just headlines," Martin challenged. George bent forward in his armchair, while keeping an eye on Martin on his right.

Zhang Ai flushed.

"We consider today's performance of our company in the range between unacceptable and mediocre when we talk people and planet. But an improvement needs drastic action. Get serious on low level of individual leaders and close organisational gaps. Too much influence of 'control freaks', too much selfishness, especially in headquarters today. These suggestions," she pointed at the slide, "can solve our problems. But make people understand that they're interconnected. You have to take care of them all at once."

"Get more specific, please, Zhang Ai," George said.

"We're skilled and efficient in technical expertise, production processes and cutting costs. But our performance is unacceptable when we move away from machine to human being. People in leadership positions are mostly experts, unable to lead people effectively, or they just love power and their image, even disrespect others. By doing that, we don't use – actually even suppress – the abilities of most of our employees. We estimate at least 70 percent of our people in leadership positions fall into at least one of these two categories."

"That's a staggering number of mediocre or non-performers that have an overwhelming impact on our whole organisation," George commented.

"We consider that to be a conservative estimate; eighty per cent is probably closer to reality. We're having a hard time trying to find any capable leaders. That's the most pressing issue we see. We did discover capable people, but they're too low in the hierarchy now. It will take ten to fifteen years before they have any impact if you keep our organisation basically the way it is."

George could only agree with them. Travelling all sites in his first three months, he had noticed similar things, although he had always cautioned himself not to jump to conclusions as his visits had been short and packed with plant tours, too many meetings and conversations to look behind the scenes.

"Do you consider Martin Fox a capable leader?" George tested the waters.

Martin looked at George, bewildered. Before he could intervene and avoid getting an answer on that one, Emma took up the challenge with a broad smile. "Let me tell you, George, how we, the members of the Strategic Task Force Next Generation Leaders, got treated by Martin Fox and his deputy when we had a 90-minute meeting scheduled with them. Mr. Fox was an hour late. His deputy answered none of our questions. He tried to control and keep us there until Mr. Fox finally arrived. Then Mr. Fox pretended he had an unexpected one-on-one with you though his deputy had told us that he was stuck in traffic. After Mr. Fox had joined us for two minutes of the thirty remaining minutes of the total meeting, he left the room for some other urgent matter, as he called it. He returned after five minutes, telling us that we would need to show up again for a new appointment. For the last couple of minutes he wanted us to tell him why our generation is not loyal to the company any more. Such are the facts. Now here's my comment: It was a complete waste of our time and energy. So we asked ourselves: Who is accountable for that waste of opportunity, manpower and office space? Was it Mr. Fox who had ordered it – or does his deputy always behave like that when it comes to supporting direct CEO assignments with high priority?"

George looked at Martin as if he wanted to say, 'I know you've given these orders, don't tell me you didn't.'

Martin's eyes pleaded 'guilty as charged'. It created an awkward tension between him and George.

"OK," said George. "Let's go through your suggestions one by one. The first one: Focus on our vision and mission. Give us the reasoning behind that, please."

Zhang Ai looked at Emma, signalling her to take over. Emma responded immediately.

"We need a deeply inspiring vision, a picture of where we want to be with this company in five years. And a mission statement that speaks to the hearts and minds of all our people. We need to create heart-felt images that make all of us jump out of bed every morning, eager to be part of bringing this story to life. Forget about emotionally empty buzzwords, like being highly profitable, market leader, leader in innovation, striving for profitable growth, sustainable products and what not. This doesn't have an energizing effect on our generation. Of course we need to earn our money. But we see a world in turmoil and pieces and have the desire to fix it as well. Therefore the Chairman's Three Generation Perspective speaks to us. But we want to put it into more specific images. We want to know how the world will look like, feel like, smell like, taste like when we've contributed to fixing it with our chemicals. To get to the mission of serving people and planet, we've asked ourselves a simple question: Whom are we doing it for? Just for our selfish wishes? Just to have more and more? NO. That's why 'leaders' with a self-serving or a wait-and-see attitude are not suitable any more."

"Nice speech … but the reality is different, guys," Martin commented, leaning back in his chair.

"Not at all." Emma stood her ground. "So far surveys have shown that only fifteen percent of our total workforce are really committed. Another fifteen percent terminated their contract with the company internally, and a total of seventy percent work according to the rule. With our current balance sheet, we don't measure this non-performance, but those of you who are in the position to change that should finally take responsibility."

Martin knew these numbers all too well but he didn't want to hear them. They manifested that he was part of the cause. He was a top manager and he couldn't claim that these numbers were not true for his own department.

"To make this happen", Emma continued, "we need to meet

the legitimate needs of all our people and the planet. So far, we meet primarily the personal desires of power-focused self-optimisers. George calls them The Egocentrics and The Heart-of-Stone Guys. So far the company allows for this group to receive preferred treatment. But why, we've asked ourselves? If we take a closer look at what their actions and omission do, we cannot but come to the conclusion that they've been destroying our company from the inside out."

Martin shook his head. "What you're saying is bullshit." He didn't want to acknowledge that there might be some truth in what she said. "It's because of the highly competitive colleagues that the company had moved forward."

"Yes, but where to, Martin? We're standing at the abysm now," Thomas countered.

Martin rubbed his neck and leaned back in the chair.

"Right," Emma continued. "But one important step has already been made. Our values are a true measurement now. Leaders who don't live them are held accountable. We're very grateful for that, let me tell you, George."

"My pleasure," George said that with a smile, nodding. He even blushed slightly.

"The next step from our point of view would be to ensure that our leaders live our values naturally, because they reflect their heartfelt convictions. When hiring new people, we should include screening candidates for the values they actually live and make this a major selection criterion."

"They're hard to find, Emma. It takes a lot of effort and inventiveness to find such people," George commented. "Looking for them actually takes the majority of my time."

"We understand that. We suggest that you look more closely inside the company, especially at our generation. You'll find people who exercise natural authority among us. We treat others the way we want to be treated, and we accomplish your tasks through and with our colleagues. We serve a common purpose, not ourselves, thereby building healthy relationships among each other. Most of your senior vice presidents exercise power to make people do what they want because the people fear them. As long as you pay minimum wages and treat others poorly while asking significant compensation, benefits and exit packages for yourselves, there will be no natural authority – absolutely none. Two or more sets of rules create separation. And we're about to perish because of that."

Martin stood up, went to the white board that was hanging on the wall behind him and drew a pyramid with seven levels to the top. Then he filled in the levels from bottom to top: customers, employees, supervisors, middle management, vice presidents, senior vice presidents, ExCom.

"Nonsense," he said. "I tell you how things work. The company resembles a pyramid. Customers are the foundation it stands on. The very bottom of the pyramid is made up of our employees. Above them are their supervisors, then middle management, vice presidents, senior vice presidents, and the ExCom is at the very top. And the higher you are, the more you work, the better you get paid. And as your personal risk of failing is also higher, you get exit packages."

"Your point of view is not quite true any more, Martin," George interfered with a grin on his face. "In my CEO package there's no room for a golden handshake whenever I leave or have to leave. My base salary is limited to twenty times the amount of the lowest-paid employee in Germany, and in my second term of five years, the reference salary would be the lowest-paid employee worldwide. And I'll only receive shares by the time I leave the company if the company did very well. If not, I won't get anything."

"But how does the Board motivate you to give your best?"

"They don't have to, Martin. My work itself motivates me. It resonates with who I am and what my life's about. No money in the world can make me work harder or longer hours."

Martin rubbed his cheeks and pressed his lips together.

Thomas Winter cleared his throat. "I believe that the pyramid approach is one reason we're unable to react quickly and adequately to our customers' needs as well as to the fast and vast challenges our environment brings with it. Rebuilding our organisation into a spider web would be the best possible solution for our company."

"Stop kidding yourself, Thomas," Martin countered. "If you'd change the perspective and flatten a pyramid, as if you were looking down from a helicopter, you'd also see a spider web, right?"

"Wrong, Martin. It only appears to be. A pyramid consists of stones, like our business units and department that separate themselves from all others. In a spider web, sure you have a centre, but it's enough to tickle the web just on one end to make the whole web vibrate. That's a huge difference. That's what makes it such an extremely efficient trap for flies or insects."

"That doesn't work in the business world," Martin concluded. Frowning, he pressed his lips together.

"Can't you picture it?"

"No."

"Muggle."

"What?"

"Egocentrics like you who believe in carved-in-stone structures and processes, unable to picture anything else and use their magic to make it happen."

"I don't get you."

"Never mind."

"But I do."

"Think of a flock of birds we see in autumn. How they set and change direction as a whole, effortless and highly flexible. I call it flock-of-birds intelligence. That's what we need to react fast and coherently to all our challenges, wherever in the world they may be," Thomas answered with a subtle smile.

"As I see it, gentlemen, for the moment we have a serious disagreement between your generations," George summarized and smiled. "But could we continue with the second topic, please?" He looked at Thomas and Martin as if he wanted to say, 'Just relax, guys'.

Emma and Zhang Ai looked at Thomas. It was his turn to continue the presentation.

"Our second slide," Thomas said while sitting straight up, "provides our answer to the question: 'What methods can we apply to judge our own performance better?' Our overall conclusion is that money needs to serve people and nature. Not the other way around, i.e. that people and nature serve money. This will be instrumental in turning this company's fortunes around and make it an industry leader of a new kind while keeping our generation in the work force."

Judging our performance in a new manner

Measure utility values

Tell the truth

Offer 6-8 percent overall return on investment

Martin and George read the slide carefully.

"Go ahead, Thomas. I'm curious to hear your generation's reasoning behind this idea," George encouraged him.

"We've come to the conclusion that the company should introduce a second balance sheet next to the financial balance sheet we are used to and obliged to produce. The financial balance sheet only states exchange values – money for whatsoever – reflecting on aspects of our activities we more or less want to look at. It ignores utility values and the whole consequences of our business activities. We therefore propose to introduce a second balance sheet that will simultaneously measure transparently what the consequences of all our activities are and how ethically we do things. For example: How ethically do we procure our products and provide our services? How ethically do we manage financial transactions? How ethically do we treat all our employees, shareholders, customers, and business partners? This balance sheet should also measure what the meaning and effects of our products, services and innovations are. And it should reveal what negative impacts our ways of doing business have on human dignity, equality, ecological sustainability, social justice and democracy, participation and transparency."

"This is way over the top! You must be dreaming," Martin said in an aggressive tone, leaning towards Thomas.

The young man stood up to stand his ground better.

"No, we don't think so, Martin. Actually, it's high time this is put on the table! We think your generation's way of managing the company is ignorant of all of its consequences, hopeless when it comes to creating cohesion between all people involved and short-sighted with respect to the impacts we have on society and the world at large. All we ask you is this: Check the facts you like to ignore. Have the courage to make up your own mind again, instead of living according to convictions and rules that you've stopped questioning a long time ago."

Martin was upset. How could Thomas act like that after Martin had just risked his career to save his butt? He leaned back, crossed his arms in front of his chest and glared at the youngsters. "You'll make our investors turn their backs on us if you do it that way," Martin said, totally convinced that he was right.

"We don't think so. The effective interest is zero. There are investors out there looking for AAA investments. By their definition they must be financially attractive, ethical and have an impact on changing our world as well as have a long-term trustworthiness. If we as a globally renowned and established company offer that, we'll get enough investors. Of course we need to adapt our Investor Relations strategy accordingly. We should offer 6 to 8 percent return on investment across cycles, deriving from both dividend and gradual increase in share price."

"And how do you plan to secure that in this volatile, uncertain, complex and ambiguous business climate?" Martin pointed his finger at them, continuing to challenge them.

"If we do away with the Egocentrics, the Self-Forgotten and hierarchical brake pads, we don't have to worry about making 6 to 8 percent ROI anymore. So far, the way we are internally sabotaging ourselves makes us lose millions, and we have no tool to measure that. If we were already able to do that, we'd probably scream in pain all day."

"And what do you plan to do with these people, Thomas?" George asked. "I can't just wish them away. There's no way of doing that on this planet."

"We suggest," Emma replied, "to move them into positions that fit their real abilities. And we suggest to flatten the hierarchy drastically, moving to project work, flexible career paths and clustering activities based on customer needs."

"Aren't you afraid that we'll lose our best people to our competitors that way?" Martin asked, keeping the pressure on. "Come on, why should I, for example, give up what I've worked for for more than twenty-three years?"

"The best people have already gone," Emma said in a rather distant tone, and George nodded silently.

"Those who don't buy into our new path set out by the Chairman and George with a warm heart and a shrewd mind will only hold the company back in their outdated way of thinking and obsolete approaches. We don't need them," Thomas said firmly.

"Oh, thank you. Good to know that you don't need me." Martin sarcastically bit his lips.

"It's not about one individual, Martin. It's about the survival of our company. It's about us being the first major stock-listed company in our industry who really makes things happen. And with that, we'll probably be amazed what kind of brilliant people we have in-house already and who will want to work for us once the word spreads."

Martin was pissed off. Did they really believe he was not necessary any more or a second-class manager – or what were they after?

"Thank you," George concluded. "I understand what you're

saying. And I'm grateful for your candid and courageous manner in which you have presented your interim findings. I'll see you in four weeks to present your final conclusion to the Board of Directors. In the meantime, I also ask you to sit down with Martin as a representative of the generation presently in power and discuss with him how we can bring all generations into you boat. Will you do that for me?"

"Yes, George," the young managers replied in unison. But Martin didn't know whether he liked this idea or not.

George took Martin with him into his office.

"Have a seat, Martin. I'll be with you in a second."

George went to his desk to collect a sheet of paper before he sat down across from Martin in one of his four easy-chairs in his office. Martin remained standing.

"George, I know you're upset and …"

"I want you to learn and grow and refine your character. You know that. Now I want you to take responsibility for something else as well."

"O … K?"

"The Chairman and I had our entrance hall redecorated."

"I know," Martin said with an empty gaze, pressing his lips together.

"Take your personal emotions out of the equation, Martin. This is not about art, your wife or any personal statement of mine."

"But what is it about, George?" Martin said curiously, stretching his arms out with open palms.

"It's a cornerstone in our new worldwide safety, health and environment approach. And it starts with openly acknowledging the sins of the past and maybe current sins that have not yet been exposed. There are many in our industry. Just think about how we've been exploiting the people and nature in the costal regions of Thailand, the Philippines and in India until ten years ago."

"Yes, but our industry has made a great effort to clean this mess up."

"True, Martin, but while the sick behaviour patterns of many top managers continue, I'm sure we have more wrongdoings we don't acknowledge or may not even know of yet."

"But that's just guesswork, right?"

"No. Two weeks ago the Global Safety Health and Environment Manager issued a confidential report that shows we operate a production plant for specialities in Brazil where we run machinery that might lead to a major incident like the one that happened in Bhopal in 1984."

Martin hadn't expected that.

"We need to expose the lies we keep telling ourselves and take full responsibility for them."

"I think that's suicidal. We'll be washed away by a wave of court cases."

"What child abuse by priests is to the Catholic Church, concealed maltreatment of human health and nature is to the chemical industry. Our company will take the lead to set new industrial standards by accepting full responsibility for all our misbehaviours so far."

"What do you think the press will make of this? Applaud us?"

"It's about living our values. There'll be many people who will reward us for being honest, many. Just think of conscious end customers, ethically investing pension and investment funds. Martin, we're considered to be a decent player in our industry; no competitor will dare point fingers as us. Quite to the contrary: There'll be enormous public pressure on them to follow our example."

Martin pondered that. Was he really such a wimpy shirker, and were George and the Board of Directors really such honest and courageous guys?

"Prepare me a crisp and to-the-point report on all mergers, acquisitions and investments we made relating to plants in developing countries in the last ten years, where we've consciously taken the risk of harming people and the environment without acknowledging it."

"When do you expect my report?"

"Be fast and follow your gut feeling."

"Which means?"

"Don't search all your files but rather go through the behaviour patterns of our key decision-makers urging such investments before they come to the Executive Committee and the Board. Who are the ones that consider themselves superior or even immortal and are therefore more likely to bend the rules? Who are the ambitious leaders who are eager to stand out and make it to the top of the company, no matter what they have to do to accomplish that? Follow that trail. Report case by case."

"But don't we lose our competitive advantage that way, George? Isn't it always a choice between pest and cholera, so to speak?"

"That's only an excuse, Martin. There is no perfect world, but there can be one a lot better than what we've got now if we live our values. Get going, Martin. I count on you."

CHAPTER 17

Rupert Hess led Martin into a soundproof activity room. It was about thirty square meters in size, with eggshell-coloured walls that were covered with water-colour portraits of men and women at all ages and in various moods. Daylight filtered through huge windows that looked over the garden, but the view from outside into the room was blocked by a large pat of bamboo. The floor, dark-brown oiled wooden planks, felt pleasant on his bare soles. Martin looked at Rupert Hess questioningly.

"Relax and feel free to let it all out." Mr. Hess patted him on the back. "I'll be with you and guide you through this highly dynamic exercise."

Blindfolded, barefooted, in jogging shorts and a T-shirt, Martin was ready for his encounter with himself. A heavy gong started the session, immediately followed by wild and energetic hand drums. It reminded Martin of the music they played in Westerns when the Indians had tied a captured white man to their totem pole and tension was on the rise. Mr. Hess instructed Martin, "Exhale through the nose, as fast and deep as you can. Don't worry about inhaling, that takes care of itself. Go." Martin blew the air out through his nostrils with vigour again and again. He soon felt tired. But Mr. Hess made him to go on and on for ten minutes until he felt as if there was no more air left in his lungs. A second gong sounded, and the music changed to a wildly bubbling fountain of synthesiser sounds.

"Explode", said Mr. Hess. "Throw everything out, jump, scream, shout, laugh. Hold nothing back."

Martin started to slowly stomp his feet and march through the room. "No … go away ... leave me alone," he shouted. "I don't want to. No. Leave me alone." He jumped up and down more daringly and punched the air with his fist like a boxer in a match with an imaginary opponent.

"Go on, let it all out."

His movements grew wilder, his voice became more aggressive. "Bastard ... asshole ... boozer ... I hate you ... you don't deserve my love ... go away … just leave me alone … I hate you …you're hurting me."

After another ten minutes Martin was sweating and felt hot. Another gong sounded, which led to wild and highly energetic drums and mini gongs beating the air.

"Raise your arms, jump up and down, shouting 'hoo, hoo, hoo'."

Martin jumped up and raised his arms. "Hoo, hoo, hoo … hoo …hoo ……..hoo …….hooo ………..hoooooo."

"Go on, give it your all."

Martin kept going although his arms felt as heavy as large corn sacks, and his throat became as dry as sandpaper.

"I'm tired. How much longer?"

"Eight more minutes, go one, give it your all."

He became weaker by the minute. There was no dry spot left on his body, and sweat dripped from his nose. He wanted to quit.

"Keep going, you're doing well," encouraged Mr. Hess him. Finally he heard another gong. Then there was silence.

"Freeze, don't arrange your body, cough or move. Be still, be totally still, become a witness to everything that happens now."

Martin was out of breath. The tension in his muscles was gone but his throat was dry and hurt. His whole body was boiling; several muscles in his face quivered. Sweat ran down his body; it smelled like the Ganges river. His hands started to jerk, and his knees felt like they were made of pudding.

After a time that seemed like forever, during which he had felt these sensations over and over again, another gong sounded. A magic flute started to fill the air with a soft and gentle melody, joined by tiny gongs and string instruments. The melody was sweet and soothing. Martin had the impression of being in an Indian temple.

"Dance, express your gratitude to existence."

Martin moved through the room first slowly and them more energetically as the music become more rhythmic and invitingly dynamic. He danced for fifteen minutes, throwing his arms and legs around, shaking his body, totally in balance with his inner self and without caring about what others might think of him. Free, totally himself, reborn.

When the gong had sounded once more, Rupert Hess said: "Fantastic. Well done."

Martin stopped and bent down from his hips, resting his hands on his knees. Rupert Hess took off Martin's blindfold, smiled at him and waited until he stood erect again. Then he hugged him.

"Thank you, Mr. Hess … it felt incredible."

Rupert Hess handed him a cup of warm herbal tea and left him on his own before Martin went to take a shower. The massage that followed felt relaxing and he was about to fall asleep when the young male masseur's hands moved closer to his chest, and he suddenly felt a dreadful pain. The masseur paused before his hands cautiously continued to move towards Martin's heart. All of a sudden Martin felt as if he had been stabbed into his chest with a knife. He jumped up, looked at the young man as if he wanted to kill him and shouted, "Don't you ever dare touch me again!"

"Calm down, Mr. Fox, lay back down. I promise I won't touch you again today. Breathe and relax so that the small muscles around your heart can still open up."

The pain made Martin's eyes water. OK, Rupert Hess had told him that the massage, which at first had not felt like one, was to break through his thin armour of muscles. But he had never expected something like that.

"That's a real breakthrough, Mr. Fox. Congratulations," Rupert Hess said before sending Martin out into the Japanese style garden to enjoy himself.

Martin walked three rounds on the pebbled path before lying down on the bench at the pavilion that overlooked the little lake. He pulled up his legs and closed his eyes. Tears ran out of the corners of his eyes like a small stream. He let it happen; something wanted to find its way out. He couldn't say how long he had been lying there when he suddenly felt a small warm hand caressing his cheek. He opened his eyes, turned to his right and looked into the face of a little girl with black hair and a bob-style haircut, wide open almond eyes and worried lips that said, "Don't cry, I protect you." Martin's tears flowed even more, and he slowly sat up, lifting the little girl onto his lap. She kept stroking his cheek. She was still smiling at him, and he began to smile as well. Then she put her arms around his neck and hugged him softly. Martin was overwhelmed by a giant wave of warmth and gratitude, which made him feel safe and secure. All of the fears he had carried around were gone in a flash.

"I feel absolutely marvellous," he whispered into her tiny ear.

The little girl loosened her embrace and looked into his eyes as if she wanted to say, 'See, its all over now.' Then Martin heard a familiar voice calling from a distance, "Charlotte, where are you?"

Moments later Selma Adams stood in front of them. The little girl slipped from his lap and ran towards Selma. "He's fine again, Mum, I took care of him."

"That's very sweet of you, darling." Selma bent down, embraced her and lifted her up to carry her away with her.

"Thank you, Charlotte, you are wonderful," Martin said, deeply moved, while searching his trouser pockets for a handkerchief so he could dry his eyes.

"Seems the two of you met at the right time –"

"Yes, indeed," Martin said in a soft and gentle voice. "Will I see you again, Charlotte?"

Charlotte looked at her mother. "Please, Mummy."

"Darling, we have to go now. But I promise you see him again,

OK?"

The little girl hugged her mum and waved good-bye to Martin. Selma smiled at him before she turned around and left. Martin's eyes followed them while they were walking down the path to Mr. Hess's practice and disappeared. He lay back on the bench and opened his arms as widely as he could so as if to embrace the whole world at once. He exhaled deeply and smiled.

Martin was eager to share his experience with Hans. As soon as he had entered the house, he shouted, "Hans, where are you? Something unthinkable happened. I've never felt such a feeling in my entire life. It was marvellous, gigantic, magnificent. Something inside of me clicked. I feel totally different." He told Hans all that had happened.

"You look different, too." Hans hugged him. "Congratulations."

"How can that be, Hans?"

"By the grace of God."

"And if there is no God?"

"Then by the touch of a little girl's unconditional love."

"And now?"

"After a heart attack you can just about expect anything."

"But I didn't have a heart attack."

"Even better. You had a heart opener."

"Which means?"

"Come on, Martin, I'll treat you to a steak in our long-time favourite restaurant."

CHAPTER 18

They drove to the best steakhouse in town. Hans had dressed the way he always did when he went to his beloved jazz concerts: brown leather shoes, dark blue chinos, a striped shirt in two different shades of blue, a dark red brocade vest and a light brown corduroy jacket. He carried a parcel with him in a shopping bag, but Martin didn't dare to ask what was inside.

"Gentlemen, long time no see."

"Yes, Mr. Marcello, we're glad to be back."

The owner motioned for a waiter to take them to their favourite table right underneath the picture wall of celebrities that had eaten here as well. Hans sat down with his back to the wall, overlooking the entire room, whereas Martin looked at the photos.

Hans touched the white linen tablecloth and stroked it like a pet. Then he picked up the napkin that was folded like a cone and unfolded it carefully on his lap. Martin had turned around to take a closer look at who else was in the restaurant, but he didn't spot anyone he knew.

"What can I offer you as an aperitif?" asked the waiter while handing the menu to Hans and Martin and lighting the white candle.

"Campari on ice," both replied simultaneously; then they looked at each other and broke out in laughter.

"It has been far too long that the two of us had an evening out here."

"Right, but it wasn't me who was unavailable –"

"You don't score points with me that way. Let's get the order out first," Martin said, looking at the menu. "I haven't eaten a steak for weeks."

"Waiter!"

"Yes, Sir."

"I'll have the American rib-eye, 400 grams, medium-rare, please."

"And I'll have the Ozaki Wagyu XO round cut, 100 grams, medium-rare, with green vegetables, please."

"Sir, would you like a side dish as well?"

"No sissy side dish for me, thank you, just good meat."

"And what about some wine, gentlemen?"

The waiter handed the card to Hans. He flipped through it and stopped when he got to the Argentinean wines. After a pause, he said, "We'll have the 2010 Catena Zapata 'Argentino', Malbec, before returning the wine card.

"Excellent choice if I may say so," the waiter replied. "The wine is just ready for drinking now. It's a blend of grapes from the deepest and coolest soils, very aromatic with floral notes, mainly violets and blue fruit; opulent with sweet tannins." He left with their order.

"Can an ordinary M.D. afford to pay for that?" Martin joked.

"The question is rather: Can I afford to have a friend like that?"

"Sorry, Hans, I didn't mean to be rude. I really appreciate what you're doing for me –"

"Good, because I've taken you out to give you the opportunity to do something for others in return."

Martin rubbed his hands on his trousers before crossing his legs.

"Did it ever occur to you that you've always treated me like your little, less capable brother?" Hans asked, fixing him with his eyes.

"Really? I never thought of you like that."

"But you've always behaved that way. Tonight, things will turn around."

The waiter brought two Campari on ice to their table, and they toasted to their friendship.

"Martin, my wife will be back home tomorrow."

"You mean it's time for me to go now?"

"Time for you to start behaving like a gentleman."

"I am a gentleman."

"If you have to remind people that you are, you aren't."

Martin poked the inside of his cheek with his tongue.

"May May has no problem with keeping you as a houseguest as long as you want to stay, but –"

"But what?"

"I have some conditions for you."

"Conditions?"

The waiter came back with the bottle Hans had ordered. He showed it to them, drew the cork, which came out with a plop, sniffed at it and poured a sip for Hans to taste. Hans swirled the glass, watched the oily film develop, stuck his nose into the glass and then took a mouthful. The pleasurable sensation of tasting the wine reflected on his face. The waiter nodded in agreement. Hans put down the glass for the waiter to fill it and Martin's glass up. Immediately thereafter, two steaks, still sizzling hot, arrived straight from the grill.

"Isn't this a mouth-watering sound and smell?" Hans inquired.

Martin's appetite for steak seemed to have gone. His gaze was empty.

"Enjoy!" said Hans, gripping fork and steak knife to start the feast.

"Conditions?" Martin mumbled. He flexed his fingers, curling and uncurling them, merely looking at his plate.

Hans put down his cutlery. "Do you need to hear them before you can enjoy your steak?"

Martin remained silent.

"You know, I don't appreciate your sulky way of behaving right now. You've enjoyed all the benefits of being my houseguest for nearly four weeks. Time to adjust a little again."

"I think I'd rather go back to my own house now."

"Really? It's empty by now. Helen has left for Hamburg for good."

His remark felt like a punch in Martin's gut. "She has to come back to me. I shall never grant her a divorce."

"Get real, Martin. Alexander Hansen adores Helen, and he acts it, too. He takes her out sailing. He flies in for her vernissage … He's better looking than you, has a lot more money than you. He's better connected than you. He and George are best friends. They've shared a hobby for years."

"What hobby?"

"They're both collectors."

"Collectors of what? Of women, of paintings, of painting women, of what?"

"Old-style Viennese coffee houses."

Martin looked perplexed.

"They buy historic Viennese-style coffee houses when they close down. The complete interior: chairs, tables, counters, tiles, lamps and what not. They were competing for them over years until they decided to join forces. Now they share the costs of buying. George has them cleaned and restored, whereas Alexander stores the furniture in one of his warehouses until young entrepreneurs with a heart for coffee houses like these come along to reopen them somewhere."

"This is not a hobby, it's another business, Hans."

"No, it's their service to others. They give the interiors to young entrepreneurs for free."

Martin swallowed and bit his lip. Hans pick up his fork and knife again and started to eat. Martin started eating as well, although Hans could tell from his face that his joy of tasting this exquisite meat was limited.

"You know a lot by now," Martin said; it sounded like he was gurgling.

"I've been to the vernissage and was invited to dinner by George afterwards."

"What else do you know about Alexander Hansen?"

"He's the owner of a medium-sized, Hamburg-based trading company, which has been in the family for five generations. His wife died of cancer some two-and-a-half years ago. He met Helen on George and Anna's wedding. One year later, Anna took Helen with her to the Harley Days in Hamburg, just to drop her off with Alexander to take care of her … Do you get it now?"

Martin dropped his cutlery and picked up his wine glass. Without toasting to Hans, he took a long sip. When he put it down again, he said, "But we have to keep up our marriage for Christopher."

"Like it or not – Christopher is happy about the split."

"How do you know?"

"We talked about it over the phone."

"Ah, yes, I forgot, the understanding and caring godfather."

"That behaviour of yours is exactly the reason why I will let you stay at my house only under certain conditions. I don't mind if you show your asshole qualities to me, but I want you to respect and treat my wife with all the kindness you have. May May is the best thing that ever happened to me, and I don't want to see her unhappy for even a second because you're in the house. Do you get me?"

Martin looked down, ashamed. "Touché! I'm sorry, Hans. In the office, things are slowly starting to turn in my favour, but on a private level –"

"Helen deserves a caring husband. And my godson deserves a loving and supporting father."

"What do you want me to do?"

"Make peace with yourself. You've messed up on an epic scale with wife and son. Now let it go."

"Let it go?"

"Yes. Give Helen a fast divorce and everything she asks for."

"And if I don't?"

"Then you'll have to find out what it means when your best and only friend is pissed off at you. And I tell you, you don't want to find out."

Martin exhaled deeply and folded the palms of his hands in front of his mouth. "And if I do as you say?"

"Then I'll help you to repair your broken relationship with Christopher."

Martin took another sip of red wine. A pleased smile appeared on his face.

"Deal!"

He put his glass down again. Hans lifted his glass and motioned for Martin to lift his one, too.

"To our friendship and a happy future."

Martin picked up his glass slowly, clinked glasses with Hans and said, "Excuse my erratic behaviour. Seems I have some more things to learn."

"Yes. But you're well on your way."

They finished their main course and ordered grappa with espresso coffee afterwards.

"So how do you think I can fix my relationship with Christopher?"

"Take one small step at a time."

"And the first one is?"

"Create joyful experiences and memories together."

"We have no interests in common."

Hans reached down and picked up the bag. He pulled out a gift-wrapped parcel and handed it to Martin. "Here's your homework."

Martin eagerly opened the parcel. Books. They were all Harry Potter books. He looked at Hans, shaking his head.

"You want me to read children's books? You must be joking."

"I want you to read what your son has read with great delight. He couldn't wait until the next one was published. He dressed up like Harry Potter. He queued up in front of the bookstores the night before the next volume came out. I even took him to a book-signing by J.K. Rowling and stayed with him for hours, quietly waiting for the great moment."

Pressing his lips together, Martin looked down bewildered.

"Every kid has read them. They know them inside out. If you want to understand the younger generation, Martin, this is a key to their world."

"But, Hans –"

"Do you want to fix your relationship with him or not?"

"That still doesn't give me time with him."

"I gave him a balloon flight for his last birthday we're supposed to go on together. That's still due and planned – actually for this weekend."

"So?"

"I'll let you go instead of me, and you can take a look at the world from above together." Hans winked at him.

"Hans, if that works, I'll owe the world to you."

"We go home now and you start reading and learning. Waiter, the bill please."

CHAPTER 19

The Chairman of the Works Council was in high spirits until he reached the door of the meeting room. He had been called to an urgent meeting with George that was to take place on the Executive floor. In the room, George, Martin and the head of the Legal Department awaited him at the round wooden table that sat eight.

"Come on in, Mr. Winter, and have a seat," George said in a reserved tone of voice that was new to Martin. He pointed to the empty chair across from him.

"I thought it would be a confidential conversation just between you and me, Dr. Bergan?"

"It is, Mr. Winter. But it might have wider implications and consequences. You must be aware of the fact that there have been media reports that I'm supposed to be HIV positive."

"Yes, I am. Damaging reports, very damaging indeed."

"Fact is, there's evidence that two of our employees are involved in spreading this information."

"Goodness gracious! I can't believe it."

"One of them as accomplice, the other as a witness. They're both well respected in our company, so it will be even more damaging to them. Unless…"

"Unless?" Kurt Winter's head turned pinkish.

"Unless you as the Chairman of the Works Council can come up with a solution before I confirm a criminal complaint I have already filed against 'unknown' and let the police investigate in our company."

"Present me with the culprit, and I will certainly make a suggestion."

George picked up his phone and called his assistant. "Bring him in, please."

When Thomas Winter entered the room, his uncle started to cough as if something was stuck in his throat. Thomas sat down quietly next to Martin.

"Your nephew, Mr. Winter, has confessed that he falsified the lab report with my name on it and a positive HIV test result that caused the nationwide rumours about me and my past."

"You bastard, how dare you?" Kurt Winter shouted across the table, pointing his sausage-like index finger at Thomas. "How dare you bring shame on our family, you worthless piece of shit?"

Thomas was about to erupt, but Martin put his hand on his arm to signal him that he should stay calm and quiet.

"At least say something to your defence, you scum!"

"That's enough, Mr. Winter. Sit down again," George insisted.

Franz Winter tried to compose himself while his thoughts were running around in circles. Did they know or didn't they?

"As the Chairman of the Works Council, what do you suggest I shall do?" George asked briskly.

Franz Winter cleared his throat. "Well, I see two options. Thomas can either apologize and resign from the company with immediate effect and without compensation and you refrain from confirming a criminal claim. Or you can fire him and confirm the claim if he doesn't assume full responsibility for everything."

"Admit that you're fully responsible, Thomas," he shouted at his nephew.

"Your nephew has confessed that he did it at your request and that it was you who forwarded the document to a local radio station first. All with the intention of damaging me in such a way that I would need to quit my job as CEO."

"He's a liar, a bloody liar, who doesn't want to be held responsible for his acts," Franz Winter shouted, jumping up and down like a rubber ball.

"Sit down, Mr. Winter, sit … down," George commanded in an authoritarian voice.

He opened a file in front of him and took out a single sheet of paper. "This is a statement made by the second employee, who swore an oath that you told this person in your office a day before the local radio first spread the news, and now I quote, "He is a done and dusted man, this Dr. Bergan. I'll have him out of this company within a couple of weeks now. Ach … but you don't understand any of this."

"And this you call evidence? It's a campaign against me being re-elected as Chairman of the Work Council. That's what it is."

George picked up his phone again. "Please ask her to come in now."

Brank Horvat entered the room with serious rigour written all over her face and sat down next to Thomas.

"Mrs. Horvat reported to me a few days ago and apart from your nephew's confession that you told her these words straight to her face when she served you coffee."

"And you added, 'Don't spill that coffee over this crucial document, you stupid old witch,' – remember, Mr. Winter? You held this lab report with Dr. Bergan's name on right under my nose." Branka Horvat said this with sparkling eyes and a look that could kill.

The scenario with him and Branka in his own office came back to Franz Winter. At the time, he had felt as if he was the master of all things, untouchable. How could he have been so stupid to act like that in front of her?

"She's a devious foreign old witch. You can't trust a single word she says," He said, fighting back.

"And you, Mr. Winter," Martin jumped in, "told me right after George's speech at the auditorium to which you weren't even invited that 'Everyone has a past, you know. And I'll make that Dr. Bergan stumble over his past. Just listen to the news on the radio tomorrow and help me spread the word.'"

"Liar, you're a bloody liar, Mr. Fox!" He lifted both hands, as if he wanted to defend himself physically, too.

"Are you sure this is all you have to tell me, Mr. Winter?" George asked sternly.

"Of course. How dare you suspect me! I'm a respectable man in this company," Franz Winter shouted, his head as red as a beet, while he was leaning over the table.

"Then you only leave me with the second option you have just suggested."

George looked over to the head of the Legal Department, who in turn took out his mobile to call the police. "Yes, the company and Dr. George Bergan personally confirm the filing of the criminal claim against Mr. Franz Winter for libelling. We have written evidence and witnesses. Mr. Winter is in our office on the Executive floor now. You can come and pick him up."

Franz Winter jumped up, sending his chair flying across the wooden floor. It hit the wall with a hard bang as he stormed out of the room. Before any of them could get up to follow him, they heard his painful scream outside. Martin and Thomas ran to the door only to find him on the ground, writhing in pain, while Karin and George's assistant looked at him with a pleased expression on their faces.

"What happened?" Martin asked.

"My grandmother always said that I have pointed knees, and he just ran right into one of my knees with his – well, you know what," Karin said, smiling, savouring this moment.

Martin grinned all over his face, and when George came from behind, he turned around and whispered into his year, "My assistant just kicked him into his balls with her knee."

George looked amused but suppressed a smile. He said to his assistant, "Would you please call for the company doctor?"

It took a few minutes before the small crowd had dissipated. Martin went back to his room, accompanied by Thomas.

"It's simple. Karin is secretly in love with George. And Karin is best friends with his assistant. They knew what was going on in here and were waiting outside after they had sent you and Branka Horvart in."

"But what about the accident?"

"There was no accident. Karin looks like a gentle and harmless woman in her early forties, watering plants while managing me. But she's also well-trained in self-defence since she had a hard time with her former husband. Now, she just rammed her knee right into his balls. He couldn't have given her a better chance to make it look like an accident."

"Huhh." Thomas exhaled.

"Yes, son. Never underestimate how powerful a personal assistant can be. Let that be a lesson to you."

CHAPTER 20

Two weeks to go before the Board Meeting. Thomas, Emma and Zhang Ai as well as other members of the 'Strategic Task Force Next Generation Leaders' had settled in Martin's office as if it were their home. Karin got used to serving espresso, green tea and water all day long. She was in a serious and constant state of shock. Martin's and her office were covered in charts and graphs on printouts, bullet points written on flipchart papers and notes all over the place. Karin wasn't allowed to tidy up anything. She kept wringing her hands, saying "I want order, peace and quietness" or sitting on her chair, covering her face with her hands and whining, "Occupy the company, if you wish, but not my office." Which always resulted in everyone else laughing out loud, consoling her with words and chocolates, and ensuring that they would be gone shortly.

Martin, by contrast, did not want it to end. He felt a tremendous satisfaction in collaborating with these young, energetic and highly educated people. He got seriously challenged and he allowed for it without getting angry. But there was one point they were in fundamental disagreement about, to say the least. Martin considered the company too large to change drastically within the next five years, at least the way the younger generation suggested it. It would take at least fifteen to twenty years from his point of view. But the young generation insisted that they were not willing to wait that long. And that time was running out to ensure the cohesion of people and planet. When only considering the task at hand and the well-being of all, he had to agree and work with them to remodel the company with high speed now.

It was the 25th of June, around 10 pm, and everyone else had already gone when Martin and Thomas decided that some cleaning-up of papers and charts was necessary before they could start the next day. Accidentally Thomas pushed the top pile of files off Martin's desk. It was the pile that was awaiting Martin's attention but that he couldn't be bothered with. When Thomas picked up the documents that were scattered all over the floor, the investment file for the specialty chemicals production line in Chennai caught his eyes. Aware that his boss Karl Kirch was furious about Martin's delaying tactics, he handed it to Martin.

"Why haven't you approved it yet? Is it because you don't like my boss?"

"To be honest with you, he's a rival for a position in the ExCom. I didn't want him to score points by getting it going fast."

"I'm glad you did that," Thomas said with a broad smile.

Martin shook his head. "You teach me to collaborate and now you tell me –"

"It's an immature and therefore still highly dangerous production process. The Board approved the investment several months ago, unaware of that significant risk."

"How do you know?"

"At that point I didn't. But a few weeks later Mr. Kirch decided to reduce costs further, and he involved me as a controller. One of the engineers suggested reducing cost by mainly using second-hand equipment. But he warned that this increased the likelihood of a major accident."

"Any idea how big such a disaster could be?"

"The engineer said if things go bloody wrong, all workers and operators will die in a serious explosion, plus toxic gas would spread freely."

Martin sat down in his chair and covered his face with his hands before folding them together in front of his lips. "Holly Shit!"

"Now you know why your sabotage was a good thing."

"We need to report this to George immediately, Thomas."

"No, you need to talk to Mr. Kirch first. That's where the collaboration starts."

"OK, first thing tomorrow morning, but you'll have to participate."

Thomas nodded, and Martin sent a text message to Karl Kirch: Need to talk to you urgently about the investment in the new Chennai production line. Can we meet in my office tomorrow morning at 8:30 am?

The reply came instantly: OK.

Karin was late the next morning. She had a doctor's appointment. When she entered her office, Martin's door was closed and she heard a deep male voice shouting, "Don't you believe you'll always win!"

Then the door opened, and Karl Kirch stormed out. He shot her a furious look and turned around on his heels, walking back into Martin's office. Karin heard two screams, followed by a dull thud. Then Karl Kirch came running out in hurried steps.

"Call an ambulance, Mrs. Bach, hurry! Martin is unconscious," Thomas hollered from the adjacent room.

Karin did as instructed and then went into Martin's office with trembling knees. "What happened?"

"Martin had got up from his seat at the meeting table. When Mr. Kirch returned into the room, he knocked Martin down with two karate blows, one to his head and one to his manhood. Martin fell on his head and lost consciousness."

"Oh my God," Karin said, covering her mouth in horror.

Thomas leaned over Martin to check whether he was breathing. Then he put Martin's legs into the shock position, opened his tie and top shirt button, and slapped his face twice to bring him back to consciousness.

"Open the window, Mrs. Bach."

"Martin, wake up!" He slapped him again. This time Martin's eyelids started to open slowly.

"Can you hear me, Martin?"

Martin nodded slightly before shutting his eyes again.

CHAPTER 21

Martin lay in his hospital bed and stared at the ceiling. An infusion solution dripped through a tube into his left hand. He had woken up in his office when the emergency doctor had arrived without knowing what had happened. By now his headache was bearable but his masculinity was bruised and hurt. Hans and the doctor in charge at the hospital agreed to keep him under surveillance for three more days to run a couple of tests, making sure that he was fine.

Martin couldn't blame Karl. No, he couldn't. He didn't know how he would have reacted that day if it had been him at the losing end of all their open and hidden competitions. His own behaviour hadn't been any less sick than Mr. Kirch's. But at least he had started to do something about it. Martin pushed the blanket down to his boxer shorts. It was too warm in the room. Yet he couldn't leave the bed to open the window as his chest was still wired up for the ECG. At least he had a bright and friendly single room, courtesy of his private health insurance and Hans' connections.

Martin closed his eyes. Tears ran out of his eyes. He heard someone open the door and the pitter-patter of soft steps. Then he felt tiny fingers stroking the back of his right hand. He turned his head and opened his eyes. Charlotte smiled at him. She tried to lift a handkerchief to his eyes to dry his tears. "Don't cry. I take care of you."

Martin swallowed, deeply touched by this little girl who was caressing him again, and his tears flowed even harder. He looked up and saw Selma.

"Hello, Martin. I hope you feel better."

"How did you learn what happened to me?"

"I'm officially in charge of you now, remember? I'm the Chief People and Ethics Officer."

"In charge of me, eh?" Martin said with a soft smile. He liked that thought.

"When I was informed about your misfortune yesterday, Charlotte decided that she didn't want to spend her Saturday playing time with her sisters in Rupert's garden. She rather wanted to visit you."

"What about her sisters?"

"They're driving Rupert nuts in the meantime, remodelling his garden, I guess."

Martin laughed and looked at Charlotte. "I'm really happy you're here."

Charlotte flushed and turned to her Mummy to lift her up. Before Selma could reply anything, there was a loud knock on the door and Christopher entered the room with worried lines on his forehead. Martin noticed that his eyes were wet.

"Dad, are you OK?" He rushed to his father's bed.

"Charlotte, darling, we have to go now and leave these two alone."

"But, Mummy, can we come back tomorrow?"

"I'll wait for you," Martin replied instantly. He beckoned Charlotte softly to come closer and kissed her on her forehead.

After they had left the room, he motioned for Christopher to sit on his bedside. He gripped his son's hand and said, "I have no words to tell you how much it means to me that you've come, Son."

"I couldn't bare the thought of not being by your side now, Dad."

Martin's eyes became soft, showing an inner glow. He squeezed Christopher's hand.

"Christopher, I don't know what to say –I'm overwhelmed right now." Martin closed his eyes.

"That's fine, Dad. Take your time."

His facial features softened. He opened his eyes again and looked at Christopher. He said in a caring voice, "Son, I feel so ashamed that it took me some twenty odd years before I arrived on platform 9 ¾ with you."

"I'm just glad you did. Thanks to my super-cool godfather and your best friend –"

For a while, neither of them felt the need to fill the silence that followed. They just looked at each other gratefully.

"I can't tell you how much it means to me that you and Mum have made peace now," Christopher finally said.

"It took me quite some time to understand the painful effect my way of living had on both of you." Martin exhaled deeply. "But you know what?"

"What?"

"I'm glad she and I can make a fresh start now."

"Talking about fresh starts, Dad: I have to tell you that you'll be a grandfather by the end of this year."

Martin pushed his hands into the mattress to sit up as straight as possible.

"Christopher, I didn't even know you had a girlfriend."

"It was a short affair with a fellow student."

"But you're getting married, right?"

"No."

"Christopher, but –"

"No but, Dad. I'll be a loving and caring father, and I will support her in every way I can, you'll bet. But I won't be a lousy husband to a woman I don't love."

Martin looked at his son, proud of how he handled the situation.

There was a knock on the door.

"Come in."

When no one entered, Christopher went to the door to open it. He found Thomas waiting outside, a box of chocolates in his hand.

"I'd like to visit Martin Fox," Thomas said hesitantly.

"Come in, my father's fine again."

"But I don't want to disturb –"

"There is no Madam Pomfrey around here." Smiling, he winked at Thomas. They shook hands.

"I'm his son, Christopher."

"I'm Thomas, a ... hmmm, a colleague."

Both walked over Martin's bed together.

"How are you?"

"Colourful," Martin replied, thinking of his genitals.

"And how's your head?"

"Ready to learn more." He smiled.

"Dad, I'll be gone for today, but back tomorrow to tell you more about my son." Christopher hugged Martin cautiously and left with a spring in his step.

"Looks like you're a great father."

"No, Thomas, just learning how to be. And you were a great help to me in understanding things a little better about your generation without realizing it."

Thomas shook his head. He handed Martin the box of chocolates. "I figured they would at least let you eat something. These are my favourites."

"Thank you, Son, I appreciate how much you care about me."

Thomas' eyes became watery. "Did you just say son?"

"Yes, that's how I feel about you. At least if you don't put me in a situation in which you make my arguments look ridiculous or superficial," Martin said, grinning.

Thomas swallowed hard and wiped his eyes, hoping that Martin hadn't noticed.

"I went to see George to tell him what had happened between Mr. Kirch and you and all I know about the investment in Chennai."

"Hmm."

"He sends his best wishes. The file went straight to the new Chairwoman of the Ethics Committee, Professor Dr. Maria Hannah, with a written report of mine."

"And what about Karl Kirch?"

"Nowhere to be seen."

"Guess the final showdown between the two of you will have to wait –"

CHAPTER 22

George was sweating when he let Professor Hannah into the meeting room vis-à-vis from his office. At least Martin thought so when he, together with Selma and Thomas, sat there waiting for them.

"Where's Karl Kirch?" Martin whispered to Selma.

"In pre-trial confinement for tax evasion," she said softly into his ear so that Professor Hannah would not hear it.

Martin's eyes opened wide.

"Looks like Peter Stark and he are involved in something bigger than just parking money in a Swiss bank account," Selma added.

George looked around, signalling that he wanted the meeting to commence on time.

"Professor Hannah, I'm delighted to have you with us." He introduced her to the others and excused Karl Kirch's absence.

"Thank you so much for providing an ethics report on the first case we put in front of you so quickly. We're eager to hear what you have to say – besides the written report." George pointed to the centre of the table, where five or six files were waiting for them.

Professor Doctor Maria Hannah had entered the room with a serious look on her face. She was a little over sixty years, with curly dark brown hair that was parted on the left and a patch of grey that covered her forehead. Her oval-shaped face was dominated by her sparkling blue eyes, lachrymal sacs and sensuous lips. Martin noticed a yellow-brownish patch between the index and ring finger on her left hand. It looked so nasty that even the golden wedding ring on her ring finger couldn't make up for it. Professor Hannah was a renowned ethics specialist with many years of practical experience in managing positions. She sat down and straightened out her navy blue dress. Then she opened her bag and put her notes as well as a box of cigarettes and matches on the table before looking straight at them.

"Dr. Adams, gentlemen," she started. "As I am the only member of the Ethics Committee so far and there won't be any by-laws and colleagues before the end of this year, this report solely reflects my personal opinion. But in order to keep my professional standards and with the agreement of your Chairman, I've involved an external colleague. Thus, four eyes and ears were at work, and they've come to a unanimous conclusion." She paused. "Now I've been asked by Dr. Bergan to provide you with an opinion about the building of a new production line for a specific chemical product in Chennai. The report starts with the list of documents I had access to plus the list of all people I interviewed, with date and time. That said, I'll come to the subject matter itself. The new plant is designed to produce a newly invented chemical product patented by this company. It is designed for the local Indian market but is also expected to be shipped from that market to other markets worldwide. The company made a strategic decision to start production as early as possible to get an edge on the research and production of potentially similar products of the global competition.“

George, Martin and Thomas nodded at her summary of the facts.

“Could I have an ashtray, please?” Professor Hannah asked irritated, as if she had expected that by putting her cigarettes on the table one of them would jump up to fetch one fore her.

“I'm sorry but this is a non-smoking building, Madam,” George replied politely, rubbing his nose.

She put her cigarettes back in her handbag and pinched her lips together while shaking her head.

“Now my pleasure excluded,” she continued, “according to the documents provided and the interviews I conducted, I've arrived at the following opinion:

A) Building a production line under economic and time constraints, deliberately introducing double standards for the reliability of the production process and equipment, both resulting in severe safety, quality control and health risks is highly questionable and not in conformity with the company's common values worldwide.
B) Accepting that some 12 workers and operators are likely to be killed by an explosion in the well-protected core-production unit and many others are exposed to possibly lethal poison gas is not congruent with the zero-accident philosophy promoted company-wide. What's more, it violates human rights and labour laws as soon as it is a known and technically avoidable risk — which it would be if it were not for the rush, as I was told by the engineers!
C) Today's pressure to come to a rapid decision is mainly induced by internal dysfunction. One, there is a lot of red tape involved

in the technological planning and assessment. Two, there are top managers who deliberately kept crucial information from the Members of the Board of Directors, making their approval null and void. Three, there's a top manager who reduced the investment costs to put himself into a better light, and four, there's a top manager who sabotaged the decision-making process for his own benefit.

D) The follow-up-costs for carbon emission under the planned and foreseeable Paris Agreement were not assessed.

E) The Indian authorities require a policy to inform the local population. There's no evidence in the documents that such a policy is underway.

For those reasons I came to the opinion that under the given circumstances this production facility should not be built. It violates the company's values, environmental, health and safety standards, local laws and universal human rights."

"If I understood you correctly, Professor Hannah," Martin interjected, "you tell us that we should only use equipment and processes that are well-tested and safe, right? How shall we make money that way?"

"Evil is banal, Mr. Fox. It starts with the small things people consider acceptable to others but not to themselves. Would you want to work as an operator in the production line discussed here?" She paused and exhaled, coughing a little. "If you can only make money by exposing others to severe risks to their health and safety, your morals and your business model are questionable."

"But our whole industry works that way," Martin said, defending his opinion.

"You have your values, creativity and guts to change that, don't you?" she retorted.

George couldn't but smile, and Selma nodded emphatically,

saying, "I fully concur with you, Madam."

"My time is precious. Yours should be, too, if you act according to the rules you've set for yourself. But I want to conclude by emphasising that the Ethic Committee's opinion is not binding for the Board. It is the Board's sole responsibility to decide whether and under which constraints it accepts building this plant."

"Madam?" Thomas asked hesitantly.

"Yes, young man?" She looked at him sternly.

"I'm currently the controller in the business unit that is responsible for this case. What do you recommend me to do if I should ever come across a case like this again?"

"Argue your case with your superior."

"What if he doesn't listen?"

"Then argue even better."

"And if all arguments are on the table and still nothing happens?"

"Well, then make your arguments heard at a higher level, and if that fails, go public."

Martin and Thomas walked back to Martin's office.

"Guess I got a serious telling-off from her, right?" Martin concluded.

"You did. But I could have stopped Mr. Kirch even earlier if only I had had the guts."

CHAPTER 23

All twelve members of the Strategic Task Force Next Generation Leaders sat in the Board Room face to face with the members of the Board of Directors, George, Selma and Martin. Mr. Kennedy was all smiles when he opened the meeting.

"Let me quote a poem to you to begin with."

TRUST

Please don't throw us

charts and rules

when common sense

will see us through!

Mr. Kennedy had the laughs and smiles on his side when Thomas Winter switched the beamer off and closed his laptop.

"See," Mr. Kennedy said, slapping his thighs, "it works."

The young people's eyes turned to Emma. She rubbed the

palms of her hands together, got up from her seat and gracefully walked to the head of the large table. Emma Cunningham was just thirty-two years old but whenever she entered a room, all the heads turned. Her radiant blue eyes, her warm smile and her fluent gestures fascinated as much as the simplicity of the way she talked and dressed. Today she was wrapped in a dress with a pattern of red and blue ornaments, and her long blond hair was tied into a ponytail.

"Mr. Chairman, ladies and gentleman," Emma started. Her warm eyes sparkled. "Our generation loves common sense, too. We can do without charts and graphs. But I guess I'll need a few more words than Mr. Kennedy just did."

Mr. Kennedy applauded enthusiastically and smiled about her quick-wittedness.

Emma put her left hand on her heart and raised her right hand. "Let's face it, our team's presence in this Board Room was highly unlikely until about six months ago. With the arrival of you, Mr. Kennedy, then George and now Selma, our generation has hope again. Hope that we focus on what unites us and not on what divides us. There's no longer the German company with it headquarters in Frankfurt and its foreign sites. There's no longer the experienced management and the workers. There's no longer the older and the younger generation. There's just one company. And we're all part of it, committed to make things happen. But many of us are not allowed to contribute in the way we possibly could."

Emma received a tremendous applause from everybody in the room.

"Why don't we live what we're capable of?" She continued with a swooping gesture. "To us, the answer is: because we lack leadership. George held the mirror of sick behaviour patterns that sabotage leadership right under our noses. And we believe he's right. We've come to the unanimous conclusion that out of the five clusters of sick behaviour patterns, it is the Egocentrics, the Heart-of-Stone Guys and the Self-Forgotten who need to be eliminated from all positions with major impact – and fast."

The representatives of the blue-collar workers on the Board looked at each other, aghast. How could she say something like that? They had learned that you only survive if you do as you are told. And these youngsters thought they should be setting the pace now? It was ridiculous.

"That includes," Emma continued, "the Board of Directors, the Executive Committee, the top 200 managers and many positions where leadership is required to unleash our true potential. Our generation is willing to work with everyone involved on the transformation of this company for the next five years. But we're not prepared to sit and wait any longer. The generation between the ages of forty-five and sixty-five have been incremental in bringing the company to the edge of self-destruction. So we don't see any reason why we should listen to their old way of thinking and be bound by their doings any longer."

Amazed, the older generation looked at each other; some of them were gasping.

"How do you suggest we should do things without them in our top positions?" Mr. Kennedy inquired, leaning across the table.

"Our complete transformation process to healthy leadership should be finished within five years from now. Therefore we'll need to replace 20 percent of dysfunctional people in leadership positions annually. We don't mean to fire them but rather to put them in positions that suit their abilities and not their egos. Regarding the Executive Committee, we suggest to include only fully self-aware people with a refined character, the necessary skills and experience plus the willingness to work in close collaboration with everyone else as of right now. When George retires from the company one day, that should not matter to the future wellbeing of this company. Sorry to say so, George. We need sustainability in high-quality healthy leadership that embraces reality and not outdated beliefs and worldviews. No part of this company can survive without the others. And, let me add, we should even bring healthy leaders back into the ranks and files after a few years that will keep them grounded."

"What do you have to say about this, Selma?" Mr. Kennedy asked, directing the attention away from Emma and the younger managers.

"It's time that our generation understands the meaning of enough. Defending the past, separating ourselves from others or any kind of imaginary superiority are no options any more. In Germany, we're on the wealthy side of life. We see the misery of the world on television, but as long as it doesn't knock on our own doors, we pretend we have nothing to do with it. It's schizophrenic, if you ask me." Selma looked at everybody at the table with bright eyes. "From my point of view, these young people have a realistic sense of urgency. We can't wait until a natural phasing-out by retirement sets in. We need to remove everybody who doesn't get it or doesn't want to get it from leadership positions. In order to accomplish this complete transformation in five years, we should assign as much power and responsibility as possible locally and put refined characters of whatever age and nationality in leadership positions to multiply leaders everywhere. I also suggest to flatten out the hierarchy drastically. In a preliminary report prepared by this team I read about transforming our organisational structure into a spider web. This idea sounds attractive to me, and with enough open-mindedness we can put it to work."

The Vice Chairman of the Works Council, Ralph Lorenz, was

about to blow up. His face had turned scarlet, and his arms flailed. He jumped up.

"I fundamentally disagree," he rudely interrupted. "We're a German company. If it weren't for its German roots and the technology we developed, this company would not exist today. On behalf of the German work force, I must insist that it will remain untouched in its structure, number of employees and number of Germans in top positions." He said down again and put his hands into his trouser pockets.

"Mr. Lorenz," the Chairman interrupted, "I have sympathy for all you say, the pressure you're under and the need to protect employment here in Germany. Digitalisation of the industry alone is likely to cost us jobs held by those who are less qualified everywhere soon. But if you and everybody else in this room live our values and take the needs of everyone involved in our company into consideration, we can create new ways to safeguard the future and wellbeing of this company. Just focusing on your own wishes won't do in today's world any more. If we took out all foreign sites, the German part of the company couldn't exist on its own any more. Please let us talk solutions, not defensive positions."

"What do you think, Martin?" Mr. Kennedy asked and turned to him.

Martin exhaled deeply, thoughtfully rubbing his hands.

"A little tweaking here and there or exchanging the top guy from time to time here at headquarters won't do any more. Although I'm German and belong to the generation of managers under severe attack here, I concur with what the young generation demands and what Selma has seconded. We either take a quantum leap now – or we shouldn't be surprised if nothing will be left of us in a few years from now. This is not about what I want, it's about the wellbeing of all of all. Please ask yourself, Mr. Lorenz, if you aren't suffering from some sick behaviour patterns as well? We have to look at all facts and figures, not just those that suit us and those in our balance sheet that we currently let others see." Martin paused and looked around, rubbing the palms of his slightly sweaty hands together. "I am an egocentric self-forgotten workaholic heart-of-stone guy. It took me a long time to admit that and do something about it. But it's the only way. You as the Board should make all top-managers in this company face their demons and lies so that they can end their isolation from others. My generation and the older ones believe that everything depends on us and that everything is the reward for our past work and inventions. But we kid ourselves when we look at things this way. We've been taking more for ourselves than we needed and have left the generations to come with little. Now we depend on their approval whether we like it or not. If they vote with their feet and leave the company in masses, it won't even matter whether we're working on our sick behaviour patterns any more. Without them, we don't have a future." Martin swallowed and paused.

"One more thing I'd like to add. I always thought that if I treat others the way I want to be treated, everything is fine. But it isn't. I've overlooked that I didn't love myself enough. I let others push me around, beat me up, diminishing me. And by accepting that, I did the same to others. I feel ashamed that it took me so long to realize that. But without George forcing me to face my demons, I would have never realized it." He dropped his head, suddenly exhausted.

All of the young people applauded Martin. Thomas and Mr. Kennedy even gave him a 'thumbs up'. At that moment there was a hard double knock on the door of the Board Room. All heads turned around.

CHAPTER 24

It was Karin. She entered the room, feverishly looking around.

"Dr. Fox, a public prosecutor has a search warrant for your office, and his colleague, who is right behind me, wants to interrogate you immediately," she said in a choked voice.

Martin stood up and hesitantly walked to the door. His palms started to sweat again, and his head felt hot and dizzy.

"Dr. Martin Fox?"

"Yes, that's me."

"You are suspected of having conspired with other top managers of this company to commit tax evasion in an especially serious case. You have the right to remain silent, but anything you say may be held against you."

Now George got up, too. "My name's George Bergan; I'm the CEO of this company. Would you please explain to me why you're disrupting our work in such an offensive manner?"

"Not at the moment. There is too much money involved. We might talk to you later. But rest assured your security guys are watching us." The prosecutor turned to Martin.

"Where can I talk to you in private?"

The prosecutor was a man of about forty years old; he had fair hair and black-rimmed glasses that made him look older. He wore black cotton trousers, a black shirt and a black leather jacket and had a greyish-brown file in his hand.

Martin closed the door to the Board Room and directed him to an empty meeting room across from the CEO's office.

"Do you want to contact a lawyer?"

"Just ask me what you have to ask."

"Sit down, please. This might take a while," the prosecutor instructed him.

Martin fetched two small bottles of water and two glasses from the sideboard, sat them down on the table and took a seat across from the prosecutor.

The latter opened the file and took out several photos of different women. He arranged them in a row in front of Martin.

"Do you know any of these women?"

Martin studied the pictures. "Yes, I do."

"Which one?"

"All of them."

"How?"

"Naked."

Amused, the prosecutor smiled and pushed his glasses up his nose with his left index finger.

"And apart from them being naked?"

"Perfume, lingerie … no address, no family background, no nothing. Just naked pleasure."

"How do you explain that you and a Mr. Karl Kirch both know them?"

"Two men betting each other who can get more women into bed … some of them we both got lucky with."

"Are you in any way connected to the Millennium Petrus Trust registered in the Cayman Islands?"

"Never heard of it."

"Peter Stark, Karl Kirch and all of these women invested significant amounts of money – a total of about € 30 million – in this company via a Swiss bank account. What do you know about that?"

"Nothing."

"What is your relationship with Mr. Peter Stark?"

"He is – was the CFO of this company."

"Nothing more?"

"I'm not one of 'Peter Stark's boys' if that's what you mean."

"How do you explain that Mrs. Petra Zornert sent me a text message at 8.32 pm on May 7th that read: Dr. Martin Fox convinced me to invest money in the Millennium Petrus Trust and established the connection to Mr. Peter Stark. In the meantime I understand that he is the real mastermind behind it all, together with Mr. Karl Kirch. Hope you will take this as a sign of my collaboration and that it will have an effect on how I will be treated as of now."

Martin remained silent. May 7th ... May 7th ... That's when they had sex. Yes. Mustn't have been all that pleasant for her after all.

He looked at the prosecutor and said firmly, "Revenge."

"It's your word against hers."

Martin's chest tightened and his Adam's apple bobbed up and down, hammering in his throat. He leaned forward, put his elbows on the table and pressed his palms together.

"I'm waiting … the score is still even," the prosecutor said.

The score … right. That's it. Martin reached into his jacket pocket and pulled out his smart-phone.

"Hang on, I can prove I'm right."

Martin flipped back thought his text messages. There you go.

"See this?" Martin showed the display to the prosecutor. "This is my text message to Mr. Karl Kirch at 8.33 pm on May 7th: "Just had the Strategy Consultant Petra Z as well. Add two points to my score. Guess I'm in the lead, right?"

"Wait." Martin scrolled down to the next message. "And this is his immediate reply at 8:34 pm: "Fuck you!"

"I'll give you an extra point for that," the prosecutor said, grinning.

"Anything else?"

"You better improve on you sex life and not on your score, Dr. Fox."

The prosecutor got up to leave the room. He turned around and said, "One more thing. Maybe you know. Do you have any idea how Mr. Kirch, who must have a similar salary to yours, could come up with nearly three million Euros in a Swiss bank account? We can't find any traces on the German side."

"Poker."

"What?"

"He plays poker, online poker. He's an addict."

The prosecutor left the room, and Martin banged his head on the table. "Damn, damn, damn," he shouted, hammering on the table. He just had had the door to a position in the ExCom wide open – and now this. He felt dizzy, his neck and shoulders hurt, his face was hot, and his hands were icy. What are George and the Board going to think of me now? he thought. He emptied both bottles of water without even bothering with a glass.

CHAPTER 25

There was a knock on the door. Then it slowly opened and Thomas peeked into the room.

"Martin, are you OK? George and the Chairman asked me to find you. They need to talk to you urgently after the Board Meeting is over."

Martin lifted his head from the table and looked at Thomas.

"Oh my God, you can't go there looking like that."

Thomas went to the small refrigerator, took out a coke, poured it into a glass and handed it to Martin. He put his hand on Martin's shoulder. "Come on, have a sip, and then we go to the restroom and make you look presentable again."

Martin emptied the whole glass and slowly got up. His legs were shaking, and his whole body was covered in sweat.

"Do you keep a fresh shirt in your office?"

"Yes."

"I'll go fetch it. And then we'll have espresso in my office before your life might be turned upside down."

"Martin, come on in." George said sternly, scrutinising every one of Martin's movements. "Have a seat."

Martin sat down on the edge of the easy chair next to Mr. Kennedy. Martin hung his head like a delinquent right before the execution.

"We need to talk about your future now," George said.

"I can explain things; I really can," Martin muttered.

"No need to."

"But don't I have the right to clarify things?"

"We know enough to make our decision," George added.

"Martin, please look at me," Mr. Kennedy said softly.

Martin looked up, stroking his own hair.

"What would you expect from me and George?" Mr. Kennedy asked.

Martin froze. What should he say? His thoughts ran wild. Claim a seat in the ExCom? Impossible – no, that thought was ridiculous if he compared himself to the way George and Selma conducted themselves. But maybe ...?

"A position in the ExCom," he said, barely audible.

"And what would you expect from me and George if you wanted us to have mercy on you?" Mr. Kennedy asked.

Martin started to chew on his nails. Then, suddenly calm inside, he looked at them both and replied firmly, "Give me a task, not a title or a position. Let me contribute to ending the destruction and misery I've co-created over the years. Maybe I could lead one of the teams that form the first intersections in a new spider web kind of organisation."

He paused, rubbing his neck with his hand while breathing out through his nostrils, not daring to look at either of them.

"That's exactly what we had in mind for you. You've made it from a saboteur of young people to their highly appreciated advocate," George said, proudly patting his shoulder. "Selma has two applications on her desk from members of the Strategic Task Force Next Generation Leaders who want to work with you."

"That's impossible," Martin muttered in disbelief.

"Do you have the perseverance and guts to continue breaking new ground together with the younger generation?" George challenged him.

Martin nodded and grinned. "Yes, I have, even if they expose my weaknesses all the time."

"That's why they like you so much."

"Because I'm an idiot compared to some of them?"

"Because you've stopped pretending to be someone you're not," Mr. Kennedy added with a broad smile on his face.

"Mr. Kennedy, I guess I'd love one of your lemon sherbet sweets now."

He smiled and handed the box to Martin.

"Anything else you desire, Martin?" George wanted to know.

"Yes, but not for myself. I think you would do the whole company a favour if you let Emma work closely with Professor Hannah and let her take a more senior role fast. This woman is amazing. In fact throwing all of the members of the Strategic Task Force Next Generation Leaders into the cold water of more responsibility would give the whole company a tremendous boost."

"And what do you suggest I should do with your salary and package?"

"Cut it down as you see fit. I guess I'm ready to adjust to what is enough. I love myself now, at least a bit more than ever before. I no longer need much of the fancy stuff I used to hold dear."

CHAPTER 26

Hans had taken Martin to Frankfurt Airport in his old red 2CV with the windows folded up. It was shortly after 9 am on Sunday, the 6th of September. The leaves had started to turn red, yellow and brown, and a mild breeze gave them so much energy that they raced through the nearly empty streets as wild and free as young students. Eventually, they stood side by side in the departure hall of Terminal 1, checking the large table of flights. LH758 to Chennai / Madras was scheduled on time.

"Are you sure you really want to do this?" asked Hans sceptically and looked at Martin, who was dressed more casual than ever in plain blue-jeans and a pullover. His only luggage for ten days was a carry-on bag.

"Yes!" Martin said with vigour in his voice.

"You've given up your SVP position in headquarters, sold your Swiss chronographs, gave away your handmade silk ties and what not just to be a team leader in a project with an uncertain future?"

"Sold one of my two Harleys as well, don't forget that."

"Sorry, how could I?"

"You know, since George's address to the top management

some months ago I've felt like a failure. Sometimes it even felt like dying. But it turned out to be only the stripping-away of the inessential, of everything I don't need and am not."

"And how do you feel now?"

"Free and alive, vibrant. Now I'm a man who contributes his fair share of repairing what went wrong. I can co-pave the way for a future that is worthwhile living in for many generations to come."

"But it's not an ExCom position."

"I'm in charge of the coolest team ever. It's so much fun working with these highly educated and capable youngsters."

"Since when has it been fun to be kicked in the butt?"

"With them, it is. Thomas is particularly good at it."

"You're fond of him, aren't you?"

"You know, Hans, this young manager can write code. He's bright enough to develop the algorithms that will run the digital chemical industry of the future. That's where the real power is. Fortunately he's a computer nerd with morals. But he also has some demons he still needs to face. And I want to help him."

"How will you do that?"

"I've booked him with Rupert Hess." Martin grinned and looked up before he put his hand on Hans's shoulder. "Thanks, Hans. Without you, I'd be done and dusted now." He dropped his carry-on bag and wiped his eyes.

Hans hugged him while patting him on his back. "You've rediscovered your heart, old buddy. Looks like our friendship will become easier on me in the second half of our lives," he joked with a brought smile. "I'll come to pick you up, and then we'll dress up for Christopher's graduation ceremony. Do you mind if I brag about Christopher?"

"Go ahead. You've always been more of a father to him than I have."

"But you're on your way to making up for it, aren't you?"

"You know what, Hans? I love playing around with Selma's cute little daughters so much. How on earth could I have been so stupid to miss out on that with Christopher?"

"You tell me."

"I can't get enough of them falling into my arms and cuddling them to my chest."

"And what about their mother?"

Martin's face lit up. "Well, she's very special … I don't want to mess this up, ever." He took a deep breath, thinking of her, licking his lips. "You're welcome to join me when I repair the prams and bikes of the four."

"I'd rather read stories to the three little ones while you take Selma out." Hans winked and smiled.

"That's a wonderful thought."

EPILOGUE

What inspired me to write this particular book, you may ask? Pope Francis did – and I'm not even a Catholic! From a professional point of view, Leadership beyond Intellect in the business world is my home turf. From a spiritual perspective, I walk the path of a practicing Reiki Master according to Japanese tradition. So how did Pope Francis trigger this book? On the 22nd of December 2014 he publicly called the leaders of the Curia, the administration of the Catholic Church, sick, suffering from fifteen behaviour patterns, which are today known by the term curial diseases. Pope Francis referred to woodcut-like sick behaviour patterns he has observed amongst top managers in his administration as well as throughout the whole church.

I observe the very same sick behaviour patterns with business people wherever I go. These sick behaviour patterns are the antithesis of what leadership is about. I also call them expressions of non-self-aware people or suffering souls. These people create a world that is in permanent conflict, destructive or even at war. It starts inside the person, extends to the group around him or her, to the department, the business unit, the company at large and, in ever extending waves, it reaches the industry and finally the world economy. Interestingly, all who suffer from the sick behaviours believe that it is the other way around. It is the world out there that forces them to behave the way they do. WRONG!

Whether we talk about a company or a religious organisation such as the Catholic Church, the root of the problem is the same. It is an organic crisis caused by a lack of (spiritual) self-awareness of their (supposed-to-be) leaders. And that lack of self-awareness spreads to everyone around them. The Catholic Church is supposed to guide people on their way towards living Godlike qualities – love and mercy –, business leaders included, but she largely fails to do so. Why? She self-destructs from within. She is too busy with herself, as companies are. She has grown sluggish from her own weight and narcissism, as companies have. In fact she resembles a powerful wealth administration much more than the successors of Jesus Christ.

As a consequence we observe widespread transcendental homelessness. The power that lies in our unity with God is not felt any more by many leaders of whatever religious faith at the top of companies. God is forgotten, pushed aside to church services rather than expressed through daily decisions and deeds in working and living with others. The same is true for atheists. They push God aside and refer to Kant's imperative, but they don't want to face the fact that human dignity is as universal as love is for religious people. Love and human dignity is due to all, not some chosen few.

Though my characters are entirely fictional, the stories providing evidence of curial diseases actually happened. The convictions expressed are mine. The holistic body – mind – soul - treatment the main character Martin Fox goes through is one effective way of curing that I have experienced myself as a formerly 'rigid psychopath'.

This book is the counterpart to Erny Gillen's book How a Pope Might Treat Curial Diseases – An Open Letter, published in April 2015. Erny takes a mission-focused look at possibly ground-breaking structural reforms within the Catholic Church without touching a single question of belief. He shows that organisational changes are possible within the existing framework of doctrine and values. He also shows that a Church faithful to her inherited mission can evolve differently and according to the needs of the time. It is the mission that inspires ever new forms!

I hope my A Hero's Journey To Healthy Leadership provides business people of whatever religious faith and atheists' beliefs with inspiration and courage to stand up for what needs to be healed.

I dedicate my creation to Pope Francis, who shows us every day that it is not about being perfect. It is about living what love and human dignity are about.

Warmly,

Martina Violetta Jung April 2016

ABOUT THE AUTHOR

Martina Violetta Jung has focused her energies on "leadership beyond intellect" in the business world for more than twenty-five years. Deep down in her soul three archetypes have helped her to accomplish that. Her archetype the Poet combines lyricism with sharp insight, finding the essence of beauty and truth in the epic affairs of the business world. Her archetype the Destroyer dismantles structures to create new life and ways of doing. It also destroys false self-images to create space for what wants to be expressed from deep down inside while letting old wounds and sicknesses heal graciously. Her archetype the Seeker made her search for a path that began with worldly curiosity yet has as its core the search for God. This makes her search for wisdom and the truth of human connections and spiritual guidance wherever she can find it. To Martina Violetta Jung, stories and poetry are medicine for our souls.

Martina Violetta Jung was born in 1963 in rural Germany as the second of three children to simple working-class parents. She holds a doctor's degree in law after having pursued legal studies at the universities of Passau and Münster in Germany as well as Wuhan in the Peoples Republic of China. Her academic education was followed by gaining practical experience in Northern Ireland and Hong Kong. Her classical career steps include M&A Lawyer with Schön Nolte as well as Director Marketing Europe with Hapag-Lloyd Container Line in Hamburg; Managing Director of Hapag-

Lloyd Belgium NV and interim CEO of Ahlers NV in Antwerp; Member of the Board of Directors of various companies in Belgium and Luxembourg in transport and logistics, ICT and venture capital. For nine years she was active as a full-time Leadership & Integration Coach, working with either individual entrepreneurs or CEOs and their management teams to build cross-cultural and country leadership and cooperation after major mergers, acquisitions and restructuring.

On her own journey to wholeness she left the protestant church of her upbringing at the age of twenty-five. She spent the next twenty years looking for alternative guidance on how to reunite with our Divine Creator. Eventually she chose to walk the path of a practicing Reiki Master according to Japanese traditions, a path free of power games, hierarchy and doctrine, but one of daily self-reflexion and responsibility.

Other English language e-books by her include:

Mighty Animals - A Short Story on Shaping a Global Company Culture

Caressing My Soul – Poetry For Conscious Leaders

Reclaiming My Harmony – Poetry For Soul Searching Leaders

Take Your Work And Shove It – Fun And Fulfilment Instead Of A Breakdown

You can follow her as an author on amazon.com or connect with her via LinkedIn and follow her on Twitter.

www.ingramcontent.com/pod-product-compliance
Lightning Source LLC
Chambersburg PA
CBHW021427170526
45164CB00001B/124
* 9 7 8 1 5 3 2 8 3 0 9 7 6 *